FORMING A NEW GENERATION

A practical guide for youth leaders

Walter, Trudy, and Gilbert Fremont

Bob Jones University Press
Greenville, South Carolina 29614

Library of Congress Cataloging-in-Publication Data
Fremont, Walter, 1924-

   Forming a new generation : a practical guide for youth
leaders / by Walter G. Fremont

   Includes bibliographical references.
   ISBN 0-89084-511-5
   1. Church group work with teenagers.   I. Title
BV4447.F67   1990
259′.23—dc20   89-28192
                                CIP

NOTE:
The fact that materials produced by other publishers are referred to in this volume
does not constitute an endorsement by Bob Jones University Press of the content
or theological position of materials produced by such publishers. The position of
Bob Jones University Press, and the University itself, is well known. Any references
and ancillary materials are listed as an aid to the reader and in an attempt to
maintain the accepted academic standards of the publishing industry.

Forming a New Generation
A Practical Guide for Youth Leaders

by Walter, Trudy, and Gilbert Fremont

Edited by Rebecca S. Moore
Graphics by Roger Bruckner

©1990 Bob Jones University Press
Greenville, South Carolina 29614

ISBN 0-89084-511-5

20   19   18   17   16   15   14   13   12   11   10   9   8   7   6

Contents

Foreword

This is a day when young people are confused, frustrated, and restless. The solution to these problems is the same as it has been for generations—applying Biblically based principles to their lives. As Dr. and Mrs. Walter Fremont and their son Gilbert have worked with young people through the years, they have consistently founded their ministries on concepts that work in any generation: love, soulwinning, positive faith attitudes, and goal setting. The reason for their success is that these concepts are Bible based and principle oriented. Although methodology may change through the years, the eternal principles of God's Word never change.

This book should be studied carefully to learn the principles that should regulate our lives and ministries. From my classes with Dr. Fremont in the Bob Jones University School of Education, I recall that when I memorized facts, I always did poorly on the test; but when I learned the principles that he emphasized, I received not only a good grade but also some guidelines upon which to base my life and ministry. Herein lies the value of *Forming a New Generation* for both the layman and the full-time youth leader. The concepts are basic; the principles, not new; but the emphases will reinforce the importance of grounding our lives and ministries on those principles that God has presented in His eternal Word.

These principles are seen especially in the Scriptural commands that the father is to be the teacher and leader in his home. Therefore, the youth director must turn the hearts of the children to their parents and should look upon himself as a minister to the entire family, building the authority principle and not simply directing activities. Dr. Fremont's chapter dealing with the family and leadership should be carefully studied and the principles wholeheartedly followed. A dominant theme of the book is the importance of teaching young people to dedicate their lives to the Lord. This dedication can come only when young people are led in a disciplined, structured study of God's Word and are then given an opportunity for their faith to be tested in Christian service to the community. I believe that one of the greatest services a youth leader can provide for the young people in the church is to give them opportunities to reach out to the lost and then to show them how to disciple newborn babes in Christ. This type of youth ministry will certainly be used of God to build principled young people.

Dr. Ken Hay
Executive Director
The Wilds Christian Camps
and Conference Centers

Preface

In the last thirty-five years, the emphasis in young people's ministries has been on entertainment: bigger and better parties, super trips, fun and games, and special programs. Parents have wanted this type of ministry for their young people, and many youth directors have gone in this direction. Teens, however, are becoming jaded and bored with the emphasis on the spectacular, for no youth director can equal the entertainment that teens can get every night from the professionals on TV.

In the last few years a gradual change has taken place. We are finding that more and more youth leaders are putting the emphasis on training teens in the basics and preparing them for Christian leadership and full-time service for God. Unfortunately, many youth directors today falsely believe that teens are so different now that they cannot be reached with the gospel using the same methods used in the 1940s and 1950s, when teen evangelism was so successful.

Admittedly, there have been many changes in the lifestyle and culture of teens. For example, the places where teens congregate have changed. Instead of the old drugstore and ice cream parlor, with their malted milks and jukeboxes, teens meet informally with their peers at fast-food places, where there is food and action. They hang around the malls, which offer arcades, record shops, food, and opportunities for shoplifting. The term *mall lingering* has been coined to describe this activity. Clothing styles have also changed.

Where outlandish clothes and hair styles are not popular, teens want special jeans, shirts, and shoes. They are still peer dominated and locked into the latest teen fashion. The dance and the music have changed from jitterbugging and "swinging and swaying with Sammy Kay" to rock music; however, the desire for music and dance that stir their emotions has not changed.

Teens are basically the same: they want plenty of fun and food, and they feel lonely and neglected. They feel even more rejected than their counterparts did forty years ago, because so many mothers are now in the work force. Only fifteen per cent of mothers were working outside the home in 1945; now over sixty per cent of the mothers of school-age children have jobs outside the home. Teens also want independence and tend to rebel against adult authority. They are still sensual and want the same things from sex and drugs that their parents desired when they were teens. Today's adolescents are also idealistic and want a real challenge in their lives. They feel insecure, but Bible principles and good, solid, moral standards tend to give them some of the security they need.

We do not find saints or mature Christians in the teenage population. After a teen is saved, he is in the process of becoming a saint; as for any Christian, this process is accelerated by good training in the principles of the Word of God. The unholy trinity—the world, the flesh, and the devil—is sabotaging this process through television, rock music, peer pressure, and the humanistic philosophies that abound in the public education system and the media. With a majority of the mothers working outside the home and the fathers overly involved in everything from sports to church work, most teen-agers have not had the Christian counseling that comes with good family training. Therefore, they are not prepared to do battle with these evil forces.

Teens must be helped to overcome detrimental influences by developing good basic spiritual habits (see Appendix G). However, a defensive Christian lifestyle can result if the youth leaders do not continually challenge youth with evangelism.

Today's truly successful youth leaders are using evangelism as the chief tool for getting teens on the front lines in an offensive attack against the Devil and his strongholds. Active participation also helps them to be excited about dedicating their lives to God and using their talents and gifts in full-time service for God. By daily crucifying self, teens put themselves in a position to know God's will for their lives.

Thirty to forty years ago, the question most frequently asked of camp leaders or counselors was "How can I know God's will for my life?" In the last ten years, according to camp operators, that question has seldom been asked. When there is no surrender and dedication, teens are not inclined to serve God. They want health-and-wealth Christianity— a pleasure-seeking, materialistic, comfortable lifestyle— instead of God's will.

This book was written to provide the philosophy, principles, and methods that youth leaders need in leading, guiding, and training youth for full-time Christian service. Many ideas and suggestions are old ones that have stood the test of time; some are fresh, new ones being used in today's successful youth groups. This book should be a help to either new or experienced youth leaders and lay leaders in developing a truly successful youth ministry and in building teens for God.

Chapter 1
A Successful Youth Ministry: Basic Ingredients

Definition

What makes a youth ministry successful? The answer may depend upon who is doing the evaluating. To some, the most prominent criterion of success is numbers: a successful youth ministry has two hundred youth in attendance, one big activity a month, an adult sponsor for every ten young people, and an ever-increasing outreach through weekly promotions and contests. Youth leaders in such situations would be rated successful by most people. After all, numbers mean that many youth hear the gospel and are taught the Word of God.

The second indicator of success might be spectacular activities. Every week the youth leader has planned outstanding programs. At least once a month he leads an exciting activity. And every year the group takes a special trip—perhaps cruising to the Caribbean, rafting down the Colorado River and through the Grand Canyon, or canoeing through the lake country of Canada. Other extravaganzas might include having a helicopter land in the parking lot of the church and whisk winners of a contest off to a special barbecue at the pastor's house, or having skydivers land amid the Olympic day contestants, ready to climax the event with their testimonies. All the thrills of these spectaculars are recaptured in the minds and hearts of the teens through slides and videotapes shown in subsequent meetings.

Another standard of success is an aggressive soulwinning program. The youth are out surveying the whole city, holding street meetings, and taking part in tract distribution and tract blitzes. There are missionary trips, visits to old-folks' homes, jail services, and rescue mission services. The youth group grows because of the great number of converts that join, and the excitement of soulwinning builds the group's morale.

A superior music program might be a fourth sign of success: an outstanding piano player, a vocal soloist or instrumentalist, spirited music, great songfests, youth quartets, instrumental ensembles, and a youth choir that travels for guest appearances. The young people who think they have musical talent see the youth group as an outlet for their abilities.

A fifth way to measure success might be the personal qualities of the youth leader. The winsome leader probably is a former athlete, has an outstanding personality, is a great speaker and teacher, and has a way of building immediate rapport with youth. He lends excitement, enthusiasm, and thrill to the group, and the teens are proud to be a part of such a thriving organization. His personality sparks a bandwagon effect, and soon other teens in the city are eager to be a part of this exciting group and to be touched by this leader's charisma.

A good youth ministry, however, may meet all of the above expectations and still fall short of God's criterion for success. Success is best defined as knowing and doing the will of God. The youth leader can know the will of God by learning the principles of the Word of God (Proverbs 3:5-6; Joshua 1:8). The Lord instructs the Christian how to act and react in every situation. The youth leader does the will of God by putting these instructions into action (James 1:22; Luke 6:46-49).

God does not measure success by numbers, activities, programs, or a balanced budget; He measures success by the youth leader's faithfulness and by the extent to which he does all things to God's glory. A youth leader can check his success with his youth group by asking the following questions.

1. Are youth being converted, discipled, and directed toward full-time service (Ephesians 4:12)?
2. Are they taking the gospel to the uttermost part of the earth (Acts 1:8)?
3. Are they learning Bible doctrines and Bible standards and putting truth into action as they teach it to others (II Timothy 2:2)?
4. Are their lives reflecting the image and mind of Christ (Philippians 2:5-8)?
5. How many of them eventually become missionaries, teachers, and preachers in full-time service?

The indicator, then, of the youth leader's success is how well the young people are being taught the "all things" of the Great Commission (Matthew 28:20) and how much the individual teen is being conformed to the image of Christ (Romans 8:29). **The goal should be to develop wholesome, mature, Christ-like young people,** and any or all of the above criteria may be used to achieve that end.

Methods

If a youth leader has a wrong view of success, he may use poor methods to build his youth group. A youth pastor may use rock music because he knows that it is popular with teens; so he has the best "sacred" rock concerts in town as the means to get the greatest number of teens out to hear the gospel. Or he may encourage the youth group to form their own band to play gospel rock.

Another youth leader may use testimonies from movie stars or other worldly entertainers who claim to be "born again" and who have reached success in the secular world. When the leader cannot have personal appearances from these people, he gets taped testimonies or makes a phone call to the star and broadcasts it to the youth group through a special phone hookup, or he may videotape their testimonies from national religious programs.

Yet another youth leader may use sports as the main method to reach young people. He awards trophies for regional, state, and national play-offs; competition is a theme throughout all the activities. For him, the ultimate in facilities is a complete gym where all of these sports activities can be held. He may use this method to relive vicariously his old high school glory days, but most use it because they know that sports have a tremendous appeal to youth.

A fourth method is to compromise standards. Anything goes as far as dress, hair, and language are concerned; and the leader plans activities that youth naturally like in spite of questionable propriety. The leader wears the dress and hairstyle of his young people and talks in the youth vernacular. He holds continual rap sessions, discussing the teen-agers' feelings and opinions, and his program is molded to their desires.

Another method often used is the appeal to the emotions. Any youth worker knows that teen-agers can be very emotional; therefore, he uses highly charged sermons, stories, and illustrations. He claims success when teen-agers come down the aisle crying and have tremendous emotional experiences. Usually this method is touch-oriented, perhaps encouraging the teens to hold hands and to hug each other as a sign of love and unity in the group. Concomitant with this approach is the tongues movement, which has a strong emotional appeal and gives the teens a supposedly sure sign of being among the spiritual elite.

A sixth method uses a cause to motivate. Knowing that teens are idealistic, the leader rallies the teens around a specific cause. The appeal to the bigotry in closed-minded people gives them the desire to set themselves apart from any other group, including other Christian groups. It makes the teen-agers (especially those from the lower social economic class) feel superior to other people. A good example is the "super-church" theme, in which the group is opposed to any other Christian group or church that is not of their particular persuasion and fellowship. This banner waving can be carried to the point that the youth group sets itself above even other churches in its fellowship or denomination. Putting an emphasis on a minor doctrine also seems to set people apart. Teen-agers will rally around a theme like this and champion the cause without thinking through the ideas. The "deeper life" theme also has a great appeal to teens; yet even this theme, taken to the extreme, makes the teens feel that they are much better than anyone else. If the cause attracts persecution, so much the better; for then they feel as if they are suffering for righteousness' sake.

The youth leader who has the correct view of success rejects certain methods automatically. Novices and worldly people, for example, are not put before the youth as heroes or exemplary Christians. The group sets Biblical standards in dress, language, music, and activities; and the individual youth in the group is taught not only to follow these standards but also to study them out in the Scripture and to make them his own.

Such a leader rallies the youth to two main causes: (1) evangelism, "holding forth the word of life" (Philippians 2:16), and (2) defense of the Scripture, "holding fast the faithful word" (Titus 1:9). Although a Spirit-led revival in his youth group may produce some display of emotion from the teens, this youth leader does not purposely use emotion-producing techniques to bring about a stir. And although the youth leader does not strive for numbers, his youth group grows as the soulwinning challenge, good music program, and activities foster wholesome excitement and enthusiasm that attract teen-agers.

Purpose

The right view of success in the youth ministry is based on having the right purpose. **The youth leader's purpose for having a youth group should be to help teens be conformed to the image of Christ (Romans 8:29), first by being saved and then by dedicating their lives to the Lord as His full-**

time servants. He strives to equip teens for the work of the ministry (Ephesians 4:12). He encourages them to confess sins and to yield themselves to do the will of the Lord. He builds character by helping each teen to have a disciplined life based on Bible principles, realizing that there is no substitute for the preaching and teaching of the Word of God. He emphasizes memorizing Scripture and putting Bible principles into action in daily life. He relies on the power of the Holy Spirit and prays for this power to be manifested in his messages and in the activities so that the teens will be convicted and change their attitudes and behavior.

A successful youth ministry requires a Biblical philosophy that controls the purpose and the methods used to achieve success. Everything must be examined from this Scriptural viewpoint to make sure that young people are being led in God's direction.

Chapter 2
A Philosophy of Youth Work: Standing on a Firm Foundation

The Necessity of a Philosophy

Behind every deliberate action is a philosophy. A man's philosophy determines his actions. A philosophy can be defined as a system of values and beliefs that guides a person's every action. A Christian's philosophy, of course, should be anchored in Bible principles. There are principles in the Word of God that apply to just about every area of life.

For example, everyone has a philosophy of eating, whether he knows it or not. He either lives to eat or eats to live. Several Bible principles apply to the action of eating. The first broad principle is stated in I Corinthians 10:31: "Whether . . . ye eat, or drink, or whatsoever ye do, do all to the glory of God." A Christian's every action, even habits and choices, should glorify his heavenly Father. The second principle that applies is found in chapter 6, verses 19 and 20: "What? know ye not that your body is the temple of the Holy Ghost which is in you, which ye have of God, and ye are not your own? For ye are bought with a price: therefore glorify God in your body, and in your spirit, which are God's." A person should not overeat or eat anything that would hurt his body-temple. A third Bible principle is praise and thanksgiving, most clearly demonstrated in Psalm 104:15. Realizing that over half the people in the world go to bed hungry, a person should look upon food as God's bountiful blessing, provided by His grace. His bountiful blessing upon America through good weather conditions and technology makes the United States the breadbasket of the world. An individual should recognize this blessing as he eats and thank God for it. With the right philosophy toward the simple activity of eating, a person can truly eat to the glory of God. A man may not be conscious of his philosophy as he goes about daily activities, but beliefs do determine actions.

The Concerns of a Philosophy

Similarly, a youth leader's beliefs will shape the youth work. Therefore, it is imperative that his attitudes, activities, and goals spring from God's Word. In constructing a philosophy of youth work, a youth leader must give careful thought to God's three basic institutions: the home, the church, and the government.

The home

Genesis 1:27-28 states that "God created man in his own image, in the image of God created he him; male and female created he them. And God blessed them, and God said unto them, Be fruitful, and multiply, and replenish the earth." In Genesis 2:18, 24 God said, "It is not good that the man should be alone; I will make him an help meet for him. . . . Therefore shall a man leave his father and his mother, and shall cleave unto his wife: and they shall be one flesh." God established the home as the first basic institution, with the father as the head, having the responsibility for the leadership of the home. He gave to the mother and the father responsibility over the children, to teach them in the ways of the Lord (Deuteronomy 6).

A youth leader must, therefore, take the home into consideration when planning activities and trips, giving counsel to the teens, teaching them, and being an example to them. Is he helping the home or hurting it? Is he warning teens and parents of the dangers to the home? Is he strengthening the hands of the parents—especially the fathers—to achieve unity in their homes? Is he fostering family unity by encouraging family devotions, evenings together, traditions, and projects? Is he encouraging teens to contribute to family unity? Is he encouraging parents to read books that build up the family, and is he holding sessions for the parents to help them to communicate with, counsel, correct, and cherish their children?

The church

The second institution God established is the church. When referring to the church, the Scriptures are speaking about both the local church (Acts 20:17) and the universal Church (Ephesians 5:25-27). The youth leader will work in and through his local church, where activities are best conducted with the local church as the sponsor. However, especially in the case of smaller churches, he can often cooperate with other good churches to sponsor activities, trips, revivals, banquets, and special programs that each would not have enough people or facilities for and could not afford. Good fundamentalist churches ought to be able to cooperate in reaching a community for Jesus Christ.

Home and foreign mission trips also involve working with other churches and their missionaries. Gospel teams help other churches and thereby build up the body of Christ. The spirit of competition may be good on the ball field, but it has no place in the churches' gospel efforts.

The youth director will encourage the youth and their parents to take part in the activities, services, and ministries of the local church, but not to the detriment of the home. By having meetings and activities for different groups all in one evening, the church staff leaves three or four evenings a week free for family unity times. A strong local church cannot be built without building strong families.

The youth director recognizes and respects the authority of the pastor by meeting with him regularly at least once a week. This meeting is for the purpose of checking all goals, plans, and activities to make sure they are coordinated with the pastor's goals for the church and that all conflicts with the church calendar are eliminated.

The government

The third God-ordained institution that must be upheld and supported is the government. Romans 13 indicates that this institution is vital to an individual's welfare and safety. The youth leader will encourage the youth to obey and respect all laws, and he will not do anything to tear down or ridicule the existing government. He will, of course, teach the value of responsible freedom and uphold the democratic processes by which freedom is maintained and preserved. Since man is a sinner and tends to abuse this freedom, God had to establish authority over man. The youth leader will stress the "authority principle" (see Appendix A) and will be an example to the youth in obeying the laws and cooperating with government agencies. Any projects, community activities, travel, or protests against unrighteousness should be undertaken with the appropriate laws obeyed, and every reasonable effort should be made to cooperate with civil authorities. By emphasizing patriotism and upholding the political process, the youth leader encourages the youth to be good citizens as long as this duty does not conflict with their duty to God (Matthew 22:21).

The Basics of a Youth Group Philosophy

Table I lists four general areas: (1) the philosophy for crucial areas, (2) the goals for the youth in the light of the philosophy, (3) the basic thrust of all activities, and (4) the various kinds of activities in which a youth group may engage. The youth leader's philosophy will determine his goals, his thrust, and even the activities. The philosophy and goals for youth work can best be divided into seven areas.

TABLE I
YOUTH MINISTRY
THE WHOLE PICTURE

PHILOSOPHY	GOALS	THRUST	ACTIVITIES
Colossians 1:18, 19 Christ might have the pre-eminence	**Romans 8:29** Conformed to the image of Christ	**Luke 2:52** Mental, physical, spiritual, social	**I Corinthians 10:31** All to the glory of God
1. MAN: his sinfulness	→ SALVATION		Banquets
2. AUTHORITY: the Bible	→ SCRIPTURE STUDY		Camps
3. GOD: His holiness	→ SEPARATION		Fellowships
4. FUTURE: service	→ SURRENDER		Physical exercise
5. OTHERS: evangelism	→ SOULWINNING		Travel
6. CHRIST: person, work	→ SACRIFICE OF PRAISE	Discipleship ↗	Competitions
7. OURSELVES: servant	→ SERVANTHOOD Love of God and others	Bible Studies ↑ Evangelism ↗	Musical involvement Bible study and memorization Evangelistic rallies Soulwinning Instruction—"How to" sessions Leadership development Parents' meetings Films Reading programs Drama

11

Salvation

How does the youth leader view man? The Bible states that "there is none righteous, no, not one" (Romans 3:10) and that all of man's good deeds are worse than worthless (Isaiah 64:6). If the youth leader views mankind from the Biblical perspective, he will insist on the goal of salvation for every teen in his group. He will focus every effort on leading each one of the participants in the youth group to salvation; for only new creatures in Christ can be trained for God (I Corinthians 2:14). Only born-again Christians will respond properly to many of the activities that are being presented.

The one sure Bible test that can be applied to the youth in the group to determine whether they are truly born-again Christians is found in I John 2:29 and 3:9. If a teen continues to make a practice of sin, one can assume that he is not born again. A sinner leaps into sin and loves it, but a born-again Christian who lapses into sin loathes it and wants to leave it. When faced with his sin, he wants to confess it to keep right with God. If unsaved visitors are invited to an activity, they should have an opportunity to make a salvation decision. Once they have made that decision, the leader will continually focus on discipleship, giving the new convert assurance and guidance for growth in the Christian walk. Because teens tend to be legalistic, they may confuse law and works with salvation, just as the Galatians did. The emphasis must be on strengthening their faith and helping them to see the difference between works for salvation and works as a result of the Saviour in their lives.

Scripture study

If the youth leader has the Scriptural view of the authority for life, then the next goal for the youth group is to get them to study the Bible and memorize Scripture, with the emphasis on Biblical principles and not just facts (James 1:25). Young people will become stable Christians with good character as they use Bible principles as a pattern for their lives. Teaching Bible truths systematically will help to insure good character. For instance, teaching the Bible Action Truths (Appendix A), getting the young people to memorize appropriate verses for each one, and then helping them to put these principles into action will develop good Christian character.

Teens must always look to the authority of the Word of God for their beliefs and practice. Learning to pray is a part of this decision, for it gets teens into a pattern of worship. A concerned leader will continually encourage the teens to have their own devotions, keep a prayer list, and maintain some regular plan of Bible study and memorization. During a month's time, several of the leader's messages will be Bible studies that include memorization of Scripture. He will encourage teens to take part in family devotions, and in parents' meetings, he will ask parents to have the whole family memorize the Scripture verse that is being learned each week in the youth group.

Separation

A right view of God and His holiness will necessitate emphasizing the goal of separation for every teen (II Corinthians 6:14-18). Separation from ungodliness and worldliness and unto God's holiness is the way of life that they must decide to follow. This separation decision will include ecclesiastical separation; that is, separating one's self from religious people who do not believe the Bible is the infallible Word of God. These people substitute man's religion in the place of the fundamental truths of Scripture.

This goal of separation should also help teen-agers to practice self-discipline. As a young person views his body as the temple of the Holy Spirit and his mind as the controller of this body, he can begin to regulate his rest, diet, and exercise. He must also learn to avoid drugs and alcohol and to refrain from smoking and overeating. Once he realizes the importance of the mind in controlling the body, he can be taught not to let rock music, pornography, corrupt television programs, and other mind-polluters infect his pattern of thinking. He can be made aware of the working of his mind and can learn that fantasizing and lustful thinking, as well as negative, devil thinking and extreme introspection, can affect the mind and change his approach to life. Once a teen realizes that his conscience is the most sacred of all property, he should try to keep it blameless before God and man (Acts 24:16; I Timothy 1:19).

Personal discipline is the key to living a separated life. Instead of reacting to emotions and doing what he feels like doing, a Christian brings his feelings under the control of God by following Bible principles and living God's way. Galatians 5:17 indicates that the flesh continually sets its desire against the Spirit and must be brought under control. Otherwise, it will wreck the life. Romans 13:14 further indicates that a Christian needs to be careful not to allow opportunity for fulfillment of fleshly lusts. God's holiness demands that a Christian separate himself from sin and corruption and anything else that hinders the spread of the gospel. Christians are to live holy lives. Yet the unholy trinity—the world, the flesh, and the devil (Ephesians 2:2-3) —is continually working against the teen's holy life. The youth leader must do everything he can to encourage holiness in the teen-agers through discipline, standards, and wholesome programming. Those who allow sinful practices in their youth group because of a lack of discipline or because of the programming of worldliness (compromising speakers, singers, and activities), are going to create a corrupt, worldly environment in which the average teen cannot grow spiritually. Everything spiritual that is being presented to the teen will be diluted and rendered ineffectual. All a person has to do to fail spiritually as a youth leader is to fail to maintain standards of righteousness in his own life and in the group he leads (Titus 2:11-15).

The teen is constantly making choices between the world's system and God's system. In looking at what the world offers, every child of God should be fully aware that the devil is trying to devour him (I Peter 5:8). The teen will also have to realize that the people in the world are not going to be receptive to the gospel or to the person who represents the gospel. He will be not only ridiculed by the world because of the gospel that he stands for but also hated by the world (John 15:18-19).

Surrender

If the youth leader has a right view of a Christian teen's future, which is service for God, he will press each Christian for a decision to surrender to God. However, both the leader and the teen must be aware that a decision to surrender always results in sacrifice. The decision to present his body to Jesus Christ for full-time service (Romans 12:1-2) is a continuous process. It is dying to self (Galatians 2:20) and taking up the cross daily and following Christ (Luke 9:23). Some Christians make the decision to surrender at salvation, but most Christians make this as a separate decision usually within a year or two of their salvation decision. It is a time when a teen decides to let Christ control every aspect of his life. Teens in a good Christian environment will usually dedicate themselves to God several times, each time giving another area of their lives to His control, but not fully surrendering. Far worse is the fact that many of the Christians in the church and even more teens in the youth group are simply carnal Christians.

Dedication cures many problems in a teen's life; he can be daily filled with the Spirit and can start manifesting the fruit of the Spirit (Galatians 5:22-23). When Christians do not manifest the fruit of the Spirit, they probably have sin in their lives and are not completely dedicated to the Lord. Usually when a teen dedicates his life to the Lord, he begins to get serious about Bible study and prayer, and he begins to be fully aware of separation. He also becomes interested in proclaiming the gospel.

Soulwinning

The next goal for the teen in helping him to conform to the image of Christ is soulwinning. If the youth leader has a right view of others who need the gospel, he will help the teen-ager make the decision to be a soulwinner. Once this decision is made, several aspects of his life will change. First, the teen may begin to feel the world's persecution. John 15:18-20 indicate that the world is against the gospel and will persecute the gospel-bearers. But as the teen begins to catch the vision of soulwinning and begins to see the miracles wrought by God as a result of his soulwinning efforts, a second change may take place: he may accept the challenge to become a pastor, a missionary, an evangelist, or a Christian school teacher. Third, he will also take an interest in missionaries, praying for them every time he reads a missionary letter. Fourth, he will become conscious of lost people all around him. When he wakes in the middle of the night, he will pray for a lost friend; when he goes into town, he will carry and give out tracts. Fifth, because of the questions posed to him by sinners, he will search the Word of God for answers. And sixth, realizing that the sinner is watching his life, he will be encouraged in separation.

A teen with an opportunity to serve with a gospel outreach by witnessing and discipling others has a practical outlet for his Bible knowledge and knows the thrill of being used by God. Christ's purpose for coming into the world becomes the teen-ager's purpose for living. Soulwinning, therefore, is one of the key decisions that begins to conform the teen to the image of Jesus Christ.

Sacrifice of praise

With the right view of Jesus Christ, His purpose, and His work, the teen-ager will naturally want to make praising the Lord a vital part of his prayer life (Psalm 145:2-3). Praying without ceasing (I Thessalonians 5:17) fosters an attitude of praise and thanksgiving in everyday situations that should be a part of every prayer to God (Philippians 4:6-7). Praising the Lord results in the joy of the Lord and glorifies God (Psalm 50:23).

Revelation 4:10-11 and 5:9-14 indicate that in heaven we will be praising Jesus Christ for His creation and redemption. Learning how to praise God, therefore, gets the teen ready for heaven. He soon learns the meaning of I Thessalonians 5:18: "In every thing give thanks: for this is the will of God in Christ Jesus concerning you." Praise naturally follows as he sees God changing his life to make "all things work together for good" (Romans 8:28).

Servanthood/Love

The last goal for a teen is the decision to learn how to love. This goal involves first loving God with all his heart, mind, and soul and then loving others even as himself (Matthew 22:37-40). If a teen has a right view of himself as a servant, then he is going to start reaching out and affecting people's lives.

This decision to love will result in a life of unselfishness. Isaiah 53:6 says that "all we like sheep have gone astray; we have turned every one to his own way." Man naturally goes his own selfish way, thinking about himself and his own creature comforts and ignoring others and God. By contrast, John 13:34-35 states, "A new commandment I give unto you, That ye love one another; as I have loved you, that ye also love one another. By this shall all men know that ye are my disciples, if ye have love one to another."

Teens should learn from I John 3:18 not only to love, but to love "in deed and in truth." Therefore, their love will always be exhibited in line with the principles of the Word of God. They must be taught the forgiveness principle of Luke 17:3-4 and Ephesians 4:30-32. To take away the barriers that prevent real love from being manifested in the family or the youth group, they must learn the lessons of Matthew 5:23-24 and 18:15-17 in resolving problems. The youth leader must continually encourage the teens to increase love in their home, school, church, youth group, and community by initiating service projects that give them opportunities to manifest love. Loving in deed and in truth is the most important attribute that the teen is going to develop, and it should be given full attention.

If the youth leader has the right viewpoint about man, authority, God, the future, others, Jesus Christ, and himself, then he will help teens reach the important goals of salvation, studying the Word, separation, surrender, soulwinning, sacrifice of praise, and servanthood/love. After the salvation decision, the other decisions may come in any order. The surrender decision usually includes three or four other decisions. Only as the young people make these decisions and reach these goals are they conformed to the image of Jesus Christ.

Thrust

The main thrust for the youth group is found in Luke 2:52: "And Jesus increased in wisdom and stature, and in favour with God and man." The youth leader should be helping the teen to grow mentally, physically, spiritually, and socially by having a focus on evangelism in every meeting, an emphasis on discipleship in all areas of life, and a concentrated program of Bible study. There can be many different kinds of activities, but they all should be directed with these three thrusts in mind: evangelism, discipleship, and Bible study.

Activities

Activities are the beams and posts of the youth ministry which the foreman, the youth pastor, is building. They are firmly attached to the foundation, yet extend above it, to give the ministry the visibility and presence it needs to attract teens. The activities may be many and varied, but all should be done to the glory of God.

Kinds of activities

This list of general types of activities is not exhaustive, and some of the types naturally overlap. But there are enough suggestions to give the youth group plenty to do. (See also Table I.)

Banquets Theme suggestions: Holiday banquets, such as a Valentine banquet; special-people banquets, such as a father-son or mother-daughter banquet; and formal (junior-senior) and informal (awards) banquets.

Camps   Camps may vary from weekend camps to week-long camps to extended trips, such as one to the bottom of the Grand Canyon, along the Appalachian trail, or up the Teton mountains. Camping is a unique time for evangelism and discipleship. More decisions for salvation and dedication (about thirty per cent) are made at camp than at any other place.

Fellowships   This category includes parties, such as Valentine, Christmas, or other theme parties; day trips to an amusement park; or just good old-fashioned fun, such as a "grand old uproar" held in a barn.

Physical exercise   Outdoor and sports activities fall into this group and may include outdoor or indoor Olympics, basketball, volleyball, capture the flag, bowling, water or snow skiing, various private, separated beach activities, either ice- or roller-skating (where the rink is rented and the music controlled), hiking, horseback riding, off-road motorcycling, and other exciting physical activities that cause the adrenaline to flow.

Travel   Taking special trips differs from camping in that the destination is the purpose of the travel. The group can learn much from historical trips to Washington, D.C., and various other spots; nature trips to places like the Rocky Mountain peaks and trails, Yellowstone National Park, or the Okeefenokee Swamp; metropolis trips; even boat trips such as lake or river cruises; and trips to the Virgin Islands (the federal campground on St. John's Island), Catalina Island, or some other island or choice place.

Competitions   These kinds of activities cover the spectrum of the activities listed in Table I, such as sports activities, including Olympic games; Bible quiz teams; musical contests, such as instrumental or vocal groups; and preaching competitions.

Musical involvement   The musical talents of individuals in the youth group can be discovered and developed if the youth leader encourages various quartets, duets, and instrumental ensembles, small band, orchestra, or choir. He can have these groups perform and represent the youth group in various evangelistic rallies and street meetings. He can also develop musical tastes by building a good record or tape library. Parents should play good tapes or records for the youth in their homes, and the youth leader should distribute these tapes as Christmas presents to the youth or make them available at wholesale prices for the parents to buy as gifts.

Bible study and memorization A regular time should be set aside every week for this kind of activity. Special Bible studies with charts, such as those given in Clarence Larkin's *Dispensational Truth,* should be a part of the teaching ministry. Specific verses on some particular principles that are being stressed during the year should be part of the memory program.

Evangelistic rallies Rallies by youth evangelists, city-wide rallies, and various evangelistic thrusts should be connected with the main activities. There ought to be an evangelistic emphasis in every activity to which unsaved teens are invited.

Soulwinning Besides being a separate, regular activity each week, soulwinning can be incorporated into both structured and informal opportunities, such as street meetings, jail services, rescue mission services, tract blitzes, religious surveys (see Appendix H-1), high school rallies, and also youth evangelistic services in other churches.

"How-to" sessions These special activities throughout the year should teach teens how to win souls, how to deal with a convert at the altar, how to disciple a new convert, how to study the Bible, how to lead singing, how to be a leader, how to be of help in emergency situations (CPR and first-aid classes), and various other subjects that teens need in order to be better Christians and better servants of Jesus Christ.

Leadership development Teens should have not only classes on leadership but also practice leading in the youth council, working on committees and projects, and taking various responsibilities in youth group as well as the church. Many of the teens could serve in the church as bus captains or assistants, Sunday school teachers, ushers, librarians, or printers of church bulletins.

Parents' meetings These meetings give parents an abbreviated version of the same instruction given to their youth. In addition, information and projects provided at these sessions should help parents communicate with their teens, minimizing conflict and maximizing family unity. Generally these parent sessions would be held once a month at a convenient time for all parents. For instance, during the six o'clock youth hour the youth leader could instruct the parents while another leader or speaker is with the teens.

Films Films help the teens to reach each of the seven goals mentioned earlier. Feature-length evangelistic films may be rented for special rallies or city-wide gatherings where the offerings would help pay the high rental costs. More and more instructional and how-to filmstrips and videocassettes are being produced for youth, and most can be rented at little or no cost. Each film and filmstrip, however, needs to be checked to ensure that it meets the standards of the church and the youth group, not only in its story line but also in its characters' dress and manner and in its music.[1]

Reading programs The youth leader should recommend and have on hand books such as *The Disciplined Life, Formula for Family Unity, None of These Diseases, Beauty and the Best,* and other books on topics relevant to teens. He should also recommend books for information and entertainment; even simple theology books can be made available at the church library or sold at the church bookstore. The youth leader who develops a reading program must also think in terms of getting subscriptions to good Christian monthly magazines for youth, such as the Back to the Bible publication *Teen Quest* and devotional guides such as *Our Daily Bread.*

Service projects Fixing up a widow's house, a nearby Christian camp, or a mission church are worthy ministries of the church in which the youth group can participate. Cleaning up the town eyesore could bring the blessing of the community. These and many more projects will challenge the teens' altruistic desires.

These suggestions from the general categories of activities can be used in a good youth program. However, the youth leader's philosophy—his basic values and beliefs—will affect his goals for youth, the general thrust for all the activities, and the types of activities themselves. In other words, the leader's philosophy determines the kind of youth program that will be presented.

Throughout the youth program a balance must be maintained between evangelism and defense of the Word of God. On the one hand, Philippians 2:16 emphasizes "holding forth the word of life." Every good growing youth group needs a strong evangelistic emphasis with a discipleship program. On the other hand, Titus 1:9 emphasizes "holding fast the faithful word." There needs to be a constant teaching and defense of the Word of God, including a standard of separation so that the Word of God and the Christian's testimony are not polluted or minimized.

An imbalance in either direction leads to problems. People whose only concern is evangelism can become fanatical to the point of doing anything to win souls and using any method to see results. They get off base because they are not grounded in the Word of God. People who are strong on defending the Word of God but forget about evangelism become very orthodox but lose their evangelistic zeal. So the growth of their youth group stops. As Dr. Bob Jones, Sr., said, "It takes evangelistic unction to make orthodoxy function." With the right philosophy and the right balance, the youth leader has the basis for successfully leading youth.

---

[1] A fundamentalist faith-offering film rental ministry with over a thousand films and five hundred videocassettes which have been carefully checked for doctrine and appropriateness is The Church Film Service, 203 Ashford Ave., Greenville, South Carolina 29609, phone (803) 233-5479. The Bob Jones University Unusual Films rental library, phone (803) 242-5100, has many feature-length films suitable for large rallies and city-wide showing. These should be scheduled a year in advance.

Chapter 3

The History of Youth Work: Hats Off to the Past— Coats Off to the Future

In the past century many outstanding youth organizations have reached hundreds of thousands of young people for Jesus Christ. A youth leader can learn much from these organizations, since they have used about every idea, method, and technique to reach youth. What methods are effective in attracting teens in every culture? Which ones lead to compromise of Bible truth and standards? Which ones produce dynamic Christian leaders and full-time servants of Christ? These organizations have found that some methods reach only a select group, some are actually counterproductive in developing spiritual teens, and some are too costly in time and money for the desired results. By examining the history of youth work, the youth leader can reap the benefits and avoid the mistakes of the past. His goal should be to develop methods that will reach youth in every culture and level of society but still be efficient and effective in building youth for Christ.

YMCA and YWCA

The history of youth work in the United States goes back to 1855 with the development of the Young Men's Christian Association in Boston under Thomas V. Sullivan. It had originally started in London in 1844 under George Williams.

Its purpose was to provide a Christian environment for young men to congregate where they could be evangelized. These young men were mostly teens coming to the cities looking for work. Bible study, prayer meetings, fellowship, recreation, housing, and employment services were a part of their evangelization program. Some associations engaged in extensive social programs, including rescue mission work and relief activities. During his years of evangelistic preaching, Moody was a staunch supporter of the association in Chicago and helped support branches in various cities in the United States. The organization of women followed soon afterward. The Young Women's Christian Association, originally founded in 1855 in London, was started in New York City in 1858.

Church-related Organizations

The pattern for youth work in churches in the United States was developed in Theodore Guyler's young people's group in Brooklyn, New York. It was coeducational; it met weekly; and it was participative, with the young people preparing and performing the programs.

Theodore Guyler's pattern was also followed in the nondenominational Christian Endeavor Society, organized in 1881 in Portland, Maine, by Francis Clark. Working as an arm of local churches, Christian Endeavor was such a success in reaching young people in churches across America that the Methodists formed their own Epworth League in 1887; the Baptists organized the Baptist Young People's Union in 1891; and the Lutherans organized the Lutheran League in 1895. Lay youth leaders from the congregation led these groups, setting a precedent which is followed today in most of the smaller churches across America. (Full-time youth leaders are a phenomenon of the 1940s and are usually found in the larger churches.) The churches felt that the youth groups met the teens' needs in the following areas.

1. Christian companionship and fellowship in an organized peer group
2. Practical evangelism and Bible teaching

3. Leadership opportunities in developing their programs and activities
4. Wholesome recreational outlets for their dynamic energies as they become independent adults

Most of these youth groups were designed for teen-agers because church leaders felt that the home adequately took care of the younger children's Christian training and activities. Today, as the homes in America are disintegrating, churches and organizations are rushing in to fill the gap and train youth from six to twenty. Yet, instead of strengthening the homes' and the parents' influence on the younger children (to age twelve), many are designing activities and programs that take the child out of the home and further minimize the parents' Christian influence. An exception to this trend is the Bible Memory Association (started in 1944 by N. A. Woychuk), which emphasizes the parents' role in encouraging children to memorize Scripture and challenges whole families to follow memory programs.

Child Evangelism Fellowship

The Child Evangelism Fellowship, started by Jesse Irwin Overholtzer in 1936, is designed to evangelize children through Bible clubs which meet once a week after school or on Saturday. A mother holds a club in her home; she may then be able to follow up these contacts by taking the children to Sunday school and church. The club and Sunday school complement the home training and do not interfere with the parents' function of training their children.

The Child Evangelism program works well within the home, but churches themselves should generally limit their youth programs, other than Sunday school and AWANA, to teens and above. Even junior churches are not conducive to family unity. They may be necessary, however, in churches where there are a number of children brought in on buses without their parents. If we believe that the home is the basic unit of society, then our efforts with children and youth ought to be in line with strengthening the father's and the mother's Christian influence in the home.

The Christian Campaign of America

To reach teens, Lloyd Bryant started a youth broadcast in 1929 and sparked the youth rally idea. He held his youth rallies in Manhattan three times a week for seven years and called his organization The Christian Campaign of America. In 1935 he made a film entitled "Youth Marches On," which he showed across the United States to stir interest in reaching teen-agers. He also started Christian Youth Fellowship meetings in Washington, D. C.

Young People of the Air

In 1931 Percy Crawford started the Young People of the Air radio broadcast, out of which developed Camp Pinebrook for adults, Camp Mountainbrook for girls, and Camp Shadowbrook for boys. Thousands of people, including Jack Wyrtzen and his wife, were reached for the Lord at these camps.

Youth Clubs

Young People's Fellowship Clubs

The idea of clubs to reach teens got its start in America in 1931 when Bob Jones College students started hundreds of Young People's Fellowship Clubs around the United States under the direction of Dr. Bob Jones, Sr., and Clifford Lewis, the first national president. These clubs were designed for Christians to promote soulwinning, Bible study, and fellowship. They flourished for thirty-one years until they were disbanded in 1962 in order to promote local-church youth work.

Navigators

On the West Coast, a man by the name of Dawson Trotman accepted Christ at the age of twenty. Soon after his conversion in 1926, he started working with the International Fisherman

Clubs, which had been founded for evangelism in the early 1920s in the Los Angeles area by "Daddy" Horton. Dawson Trotman gained many of his ideas and experiences working with and training leaders for these boys' clubs. In 1933 he started working with sailors, and in 1935 he started the Navigators organization, which spread to all the armed services by 1942. An account of the growth of this organization is given by Betty Skinner in her book entitled *Daws,* a biography of Dawson Trotman.

The significant work of this organization was a well-defined discipleship program. Within twenty-four hours of conversion, the soulwinner began his follow-up program with his convert and met with him once a week thereafter. His first step was to get the convert involved in a Bible memory program, then teach him how to fellowship with the Lord through prayer and obedience to the Word, and then get him witnessing to and discipling others. To Daws it was the worst of all errors to leave a new convert without follow-up and discipling. Trotman drowned in 1956 at Schroon Lake, New York, but his organization thrived. Though now given to ecumenical compromise, Navigators is still known for its Bible study and Bible memory work and its individual discipleship.

Christian Service Brigade and Pioneer Girls

In 1937, the Christian Service Brigade for boys was started by Joe Coughlin. Structured somewhat like Cub and Boy Scouts, it had a great appeal to the junior high and senior high boys. Its female counterpart, Pioneer Girls, was founded in 1939 by Carol Erickson.

Word of Life

Jack Wyrtzen and his wife got their idea of reaching youth from Percy Crawford. They started their Word of Life radio broadcast in 1940 and held weekly youth rallies which attracted many servicemen. Wyrtzen's rallies featured peppy music, punchy youth testimonies, and rousing evangelistic sermons, which were coupled with Wyrtzen's infectious enthusiasm and positive attitudes of faith. These rallies attracted youth by the thousands. His spirit stirred up the evangelistically minded Christians, and seven times in 1944 he filled Madison Square Garden with 20,000 people. At one rally he had 10,000 standing outside. In 1948 he held a one-night rally in Yankee Stadium with 40,000 present and 1,100 conversions.

His camp ministry started in 1947 with the purchase of an island in Schroon Lake, New York. Now there are four camps—the island for teens, a ranch, a tent and trailer camp, and an inn for adults—where over 20,000 campers are ministered to each year. He has recently opened a new camp in Florida. In 1970 he opened a one-year Bible school at the ranch to train youth and laymen in the Bible for evangelism, camp work, and the ministry. His missionary program consists of thirteen overseas camps and seven foreign Bible institutes.

When Jack Wyrtzen had the vision for a club ministry, he asked Paul Bubar to start the program in 1959. By 1988 they had hundreds of teen clubs, career fellowship clubs, and Olympian clubs (for ages 6-12). (See Harry Bollback's book, *The House That God Built.*)

Many fundamentalists do not agree with the music standards of Word of Life, some of the speakers they use at their camps, nor the places Word of Life staff members speak.

Young Life Campaign

The gospel youth club idea was further promoted by Jim Rayburn in 1937 while he was a student at Dallas Theological Seminary. In England Arthur Wood with his brother Fredrick started the National Young Life Campaign in 1911. Arthur then came to America and with Lloyd Bryant challenged Christians to reach youth. Jim Rayburn was inspired by him to start youth clubs, and after graduation in 1941 he started Young Life Campaign in Dallas, Texas. Rayburn had an unusual approach to teen-agers as detailed in Charles

Meredith's book, *It's a Sin to Bore a Kid: The Story of Young Life*.

One of Rayburn's main themes was unconditional friendliness (accepting teens as they are) in order to win a right to be heard. "Go where the kids are (school grounds, hangouts, ball practice, and so on)," he said, "and show your love and friendliness. Most teens feel rejected and friendless, and the club leader becomes a real friend to whom they will eventually listen."

A second principle in reaching youth was to make the gospel and Jesus Christ very real and exciting. "Give out the gospel in a conversational style in the vocabulary of the teens," he challenged, "for it is a sin to bore a kid with the gospel."

A third idea was to find a neutral, informal setting for club meetings, preferably in a living room with teens sitting on the floor. Meetings were held on weekday evenings, and the club leaders capitalized on good humor and music to establish an openness to the gospel. The messages communicated the certainties of the Word of God and never doubts, and Jesus Christ was exalted in every message.

A fourth principle, one new with Young Life, was to go after the leaders. Since teens follow leaders, the football captain, the head cheerleader, and the class president were targets to get to the meetings; the others would follow along.

A fifth principle was to build on the young people's instinct for adventure by having isolated resort-style camps programmed for adventure and discovery. Counselor-centered camps were so successful that Young Life now has eleven camps in various parts of the United States and two overseas.

Young Life was also one of the first groups to have the two-pronged approach to youth, reaching sinners in their club meetings and discipling the converts in their campaigner meetings held on a separate night. The organization became neo-evangelical in the fifties and somewhat influenced by neo-orthodox theology in later years. Jim Rayburn retired in 1964 because of poor health and died in 1970; Bill Starr was then appointed director of Young Life.

Youth for Christ

The rally approach to teens reached full fruition in the Youth for Christ organization. After a big Chicago rally drawing 30,000 people on October 21, 1944, a temporary committee for Youth for Christ International was formed with Torrey Johnson as chairman. On June 1, 1945, a rally in Chicago's Soldier Field drew 75,000 people, and the Youth for Christ International was officially incorporated that year. This rally was an example of the type of flamboyancy that seemed to attract youth and characterized YFC tactics. James Hefley's book on the history of Youth for Christ, *God Goes to High School,* describes that rally:

(1) A 5000-voice white-robed choir;
(2) 500 nurses in uniform forming a living white cross on the platform;
(3) Testimonies from outstanding people;
(4) A sports appeal with Gil Dodds, the champion miler, running a few laps around the track;
(5) Rousing evangelistic singing and heart-touching solos with a 300-piece band and eight pianos;
(6) An outstanding popular speaker (Percy Crawford) who could speak on the teens' level from the Word of God;
(7) An invitation giving teens a chance to be dealt with personally.

The rallies were always highly publicized in newspapers, by handout leaflets, and with banners across the streets and on buildings, sporting their slogan: "Geared to the times and anchored to the Rock."

Actually, the first rally named Youth for Christ, which attracted 500 teens, was held in Canada in 1934 by Paul Guiness. Oscar Guilliams, who had a broadcast and rally in Southern California, started a similar rally in Detroit in 1937 called the Voice of Christian Youth. Al Metsker started his rallies in Kansas City in 1943 and called them Singspiration. The first United States rally called Youth for

Christ was started by Roger Malsbury in Indianapolis in 1943. In 1944 Dick Harvey was holding YFC rallies in St. Louis.

It was Al Metsker who, in 1943 with the help of a teen-ager named Judy Raby, started the first YFC Bible clubs that supplemented the rallies. When the school board refused permission to meet on school grounds in 1944, this club and others after it started using mobile chapels (buses fixed up as chapels). The Bible club idea spread to other cities, where clubs were held in local high schools.

These Bible clubs were oriented to teach Christians soulwinning and the Bible. The Bible Quiz became a standard inter-club competition and culminated in national championships every summer at the YFC convention at Winona Lake. Talent contests also were a regular feature at the convention. The clubs then fed into the city-wide rallies on Saturday nights.

In this organization also the two-pronged approach to teens developed: the Saturday night rally to convert sinners and the Bible club to train Christians. By 1947, eight hundred Saturday night rallies were going on in cities across America and around the world. In 1950 Jack Hamilton, who had been Al Metsker's assistant, got the Bible clubs going on a national basis; and by 1955, 2,000 clubs were meeting each week. In 1956 there were 33,000 decisions for Christ in the rallies and 20,000 decisions in the clubs.

The organization later became neo-evangelical to the point that Warren Wiersbe, a former editor of the YFC magazine, commented: "YFC was geared to the times and anchored to the Rock, but the anchor was beginning to slip." The organization got so far away from its original thrust that Al Metsker, himself an evangelical, pulled the Kansas City group out in 1970 to form the Youth Evangelism Association. He wanted to get the rallies back to the "Percy Crawford-style" of dynamic, evangelistic Bible preaching that had characterized the early days of YFC. In 1976 he started his Christ Unlimited Bible Institute, a twelve-month youth leadership training program. In 1977 he started the Associated

Ministries, reaching out to start rallies in twenty other cities in the United States.

After seeing the fantastic success of YFC, the Southern Baptists in Texas used the rally method in the late forties and early fifties, promoting weekly rallies called "Adventurers for Christ." Several other organizations started discipleship clubs in New York City, New Jersey, and Chicago.

AWANA

The AWANA clubs, first called the White Shirt Brigade under Lance Lathan, began their development in Chicago in the thirties; the organization was officially incorporated in 1950. The clubs had been developed for children in grades three through eight; however, a coed teen-age club with a nautical theme was added later and called Shipmates. This kind of club was a program that the local churches developed themselves using the national AWANA curriculum, format, and materials. The program has been very successful, reaching into over 7,000 churches.

Neighborhood Bible Time

Charles Homsher started working with children in the slums of Denver in 1952. He held one-hour Bible classes on a bus parked under a shade tree in the neighborhood. He held weekday classes after school for a follow-up program, and by 1954 he was reaching teens with these classes. As the work grew, he called it Mobile Bible Time and later changed the name to Neighborhood Bible Time. In addition, in 1956, he started holding Bible classes and revivals in churches. In 1965 he went nationwide, and by 1982 he was holding 169 crusades with thirty-five evangelists, seventeen of them teen evangelists. For the children's crusades, he uses a high degree of competition and reinforcement by awarding ribbons that every child can earn. The crusades are held in local churches mainly in the summer months; in many cases they take the place of daily vacation Bible school. In 1983 he also started holding weekend teen revivals throughout the year.

Youth Ranches

Florida Bible College started Youth Ranches in Southern Florida in 1962. These backyard Bible clubs for teens follow the format that Youth for Christ used in its clubs. They were reaching over 200 areas in Florida at one point. Some graduates have started Youth Ranches in other parts of the United States.

Pro-Teens

In Rocky Mount, North Carolina, in 1969, Frank Hamrick developed special clubs designed to serve as the young people's Sunday night youth meeting in the local church. These were designed very much like the original Christian Endeavor groups. The strong points of the fundamentalist Pro-Teen program (which at one time had over 500 clubs) are the in-depth Bible study curriculum to build Christian character and the challenging programs of practical assignments to motivate the youth in evangelism.

HI BA Clubs

In 1939 Brandt Reed held his first club meeting for Christian teens, designed to disciple and train Christians to evangelize their friends in high school. By 1944 the High School Evangelism Fellowship was incorporated and developed into a network of clubs in the metropolitan areas of New York and New Jersey. They were called High School Born-Again Clubs (HI BA clubs). An overseas work in Japan was started by missionary Ken Clark, developing into twenty clubs. In 1974 this work was turned over to the Japanese who had been trained in the clubs. When Reed died in March of 1982, Clark took over as International Director. This evangelical organization has cooperated in the follow-up work of the Graham Crusades and has a yearly miniature Urbana Missionary Conference for high schoolers. To date they have over a hundred missionaries on the field as a result of these conferences.

Hi-C Clubs

In 1932 Virginia Stevens started a Miracle Book Club for teens in Chicago. Similar clubs had previously been started in Columbus, Georgia, under the direction of a Mrs. McCluskey. From 1936 to 1943, under the Christian Teacher's Fellowship, the club grew and became the Hi-Crusader Clubs in 1943. Don Ankerburg became director in the fifties. Bill Gothard was a club leader and became director of the clubs in 1959, when the clubs had grown to fifty in number and were reaching several thousand teens each week. After getting a new director in 1963, this club work was finally disbanded in 1965. Out of this work the concept of campus teams was developed and later became the Institute in Basic Youth Conflicts. The name was later changed to Institute in Basic Life Principles.

Institute in Basic Life Principles

Bill Gothard began successfully working with teen street gangs in the inner city in 1963. However, in evaluating over five hundred converts, he could not see any progress in their development as full-time servants of Christ. On the basis of Malachi 4:6—"And he shall turn the heart of the fathers to the children, and the heart of the children to their fathers"— he changed his whole approach. Seeing that the best way to reach the teens was by training the fathers, he started his Youth Conflicts seminars in 1965, reaching youth pastors with the new approach. The youth pastors and Christian adults who found solutions to their own conflicts in the principles of the Word of God urged their friends to attend. Their word-of-mouth recommendations resulted in seminars all over the country to train youth and parents in Bible principles. Whole families attend the seminars, but the emphasis is on the fathers' fulfilling their God-ordained training function (Ephesians 6:4).

The emphasis on building families by training fathers has been promoted in many churches across the United States as a result of the Gothard seminars. Many churches are now having yearly family conferences, and many camps are now holding regular couples retreats and family camps.

College and Career Outreach

Other works which must be considered in the historical perspective on youth ministries are the organizations that have been developed to reach the upper end of the teen-age bracket, the college and career group.

Inter-Varsity Fellowship

The first real attempt to reach the college age was the Inter-Varsity Fellowship of America, founded in England in 1928 and brought to the United States in 1941. Theirs was the Bible-study approach for Christian students, fortifying them with Bible knowledge and encouraging them to be testimonies for the Lord. Inter-Varsity has a strong missionary emphasis, climaxing each year at the ecumenical Urbana, Illinois, missionary conference.

Campus Crusade for Christ

In 1951 Bill Bright started the Campus Crusade for Christ. He originated the survey approach, with his four spiritual laws as an evangelistic tool, and followed up with dormitory Bible studies. Later he also used the rally approach several times a year on the campus, bringing in qualified speakers to give an intellectual evangelistic emphasis. The organization is now on hundreds of campuses and is known for being evangelistic though ecumenical in its approach. The high school outreach of Campus Crusade is the recently organized Student Venture program under the direction of Chuck Klein.

Fellowship of Christian Athletes

The Fellowship of Christian Athletes was started in 1954 by Don McClanen. Local clubs used the testimonies and personal witnesses of outstanding athletes to teammates as their main tool to reach sinners. Some well-known college and professional teams have had a majority of Christian players who have prayer before games and organize Bible studies with most of the team attending. They now have a number of clubs in high schools all over the country. These fellowships tend to become ecumenical in their attempts to reach all the athletes of various ball teams.

Campus Bible Fellowship

Hal Miller spearheaded Baptist Mid-Missions's effort to reach the college-age student by launching the fundamentalist counterpart to Inter-Varsity, which had by that time become very ecumenical. The Campus Bible Fellowship was begun in 1965.

Real Life Ministries

Another fundamentalist campus organization following the pattern of Campus Crusade is the Real Life Ministries, started by Terry Herbert in 1970 under the name of the Forever Generation. Leadership training is the key to their expansion, and they try to work out of a fundamentalist independent church near the campus. Their program uses dormitory Bible studies as the point of contact and a sound discipling program as the key to growth.

Lessons for the Present

Since 1960 the direction of youth work has been away from parachurch organizations and focused on youth groups within the local church. As more and more churches grew to over four hundred with an outreach through a good bus ministry, teens would sometimes constitute twenty per cent of the total church attendance. Full-time youth leaders were hired by some churches to minister to this expanding young membership. However, the majority of youth leaders in the churches still are lay leaders.

When the Christian schools drew the majority of Christian teen-agers out of the public schools, the former contacts that the parachurch organization had been using to reach the unsaved public school teens evaporated. Therefore, since the early sixties there has been a shift to the local church youth group, with major publishing houses supplying materials, programs, and ideas directed to this growing clientele.

The above history shows a pattern of ministry styles and methodology to which teens respond best. A forty-year cycle appears—from the avant-garde approach to the conservative and back again. The twenties can be compared to the sixties, the thirties to the seventies, the forties to the eighties, and so on. Using this model, it is possible to predict with good probability that the youth of the nineties will respond well to rallies and club work as they did in the fifties. But the youth leader should also see some important general principles about reaching teens with the gospel that will work in any decade.

(1) It is best to work in and through the church, God's ordained vehicle for reaching and developing people for service. If the organization is independent of the church and does not see the need to work through it, then the teen is drawn from the church and becomes alienated from it. The young person then has no place to turn for spiritual help after he graduates or moves out of the age bracket of the organization.

(2) A church youth group can effectively use the club approach since teens like the informal camaraderie of meeting in a home or other neutral setting in the evening for activities, skits, music, and food, along with the challenge of studying Bible principles needed for life. The church can decide to let the youth meet in the youth facility during the midweek service, or the youth can meet in a home another night of the week. Public school Bible clubs (see Appendix J) meeting in the early morning or evening at a member's home and run by the youth leader can be an effective evangelistic tool and a good contact with unsaved teens. A career club for high school graduates that features Bible study and evangelism will reach this group and also meet their social needs.

(3) The youth evangelistic rally or other activity to reach sinners can be held by the youth group at least once a month

or even every Saturday night. A lively music program with a good pianist, short fresh testimonies (of blessing, overcoming temptation, and witnessing experiences), and dynamic evangelistic sermons in the language of, and related to, the teens' everyday lives are essential ingredients in this type of meeting. Small churches can join with other churches of like faith and practice since a good crowd is essential for the excitement and bandwagon effect of a rally.

(4) A camping program should be a vital part of a youth ministry since about a third of the salvation or dedication decisions are made at camp. Most churches use organized camps, especially for week-long camping. Some rent state park facilities or commercial camps and hold their own camp. Wilderness camping, canoe trips, and even private beach and lake camping are becoming popular means to reach teens.

(5) A weekly radio program for teens can be a very effective tool for a youth group to use. This can be a half-hour or hour rebroadcast of part of the Saturday night rally or a special program incorporating all the features of a good rally. A question-and-answer time can also be a part of the program.

(6) Unconditional friendliness and enthusiasm are the two things that appeal most to teens and make them want to come to the youth meetings and activities. Not only the leader but also the youth group members themselves must exhibit God's love and eagerly reach out to the lost and friendless teens. Teens are looking for friends and excitement, and a good youth group must provide it. A warm, loving social group full of enthusiasm, excitement, activity, and love will succeed in reaching teens.

(7) The youth leader must work to reach fathers and strengthen the parents' ministry with their families. Activities and programs must never interfere with family unity. Strong Christian homes are the greatest factor in helping the teen develop into a Christian leader and full-time servant. The wise youth leader will develop his contact with the parents through training meetings, activities, and conferences.

The youth leader must be creative in his approach to teens within the confines of Bible principles. Obviously, he must respect the church culture within which he is working. However, he can still be innovative in his approach and outreach as long as no Bible principles are being violated and the pastor approves. He also must work with the parents, who have the responsibility and control over their teens. If he offends or upsets the parents or the church officials, he is not going to reach many teens. Keeping the parents and the pastor fully informed as to what he has planned—and why—will make a difference in the response to his program.

Chapter 4
The Junior High Years: Tranquility to Upheaval

Working effectively with teens requires a knowledge of the changes that all teens experience and how these changes affect the various areas of their lives. The youth leader must adapt his program and ministry to meet the needs arising from these changes. Behavior is affected to a great extent by the way a teen reacts to change, and his reaction becomes so typical that a leader or a parent can almost predict what kind of behavior to expect in the teen years.

Signs

Junior high students are at the age when the greatest changes of their lives are taking place. These changes are mainly physical, but they affect the young person's emotional and social life as well as his intellectual and spiritual responses. During the junior high years comes a period of pubescence, which occurs at the end of childhood and in the first part of adolescence. Young people know that they are in this period of pubescence by two specific developments.

The first is a sudden spurt of growth, perhaps three to six inches in an eight- to twelve-month period of time. This change can be upsetting to a girl in the fifth grade who is taller than all of the other girls and boys. She may experience some anxiety as she reaches and passes the five-foot mark and wonders whether she will ever stop growing. Usually after this extreme growth in height, which makes the average teen look like a string bean, the young person begins to put on weight and to fill out to normal proportions.

A second sign of pubescence is the maturation of the sex organs. Girls' breasts begin to develop; soon afterward their periods begin, though these may be irregular during the first year. For boys, the sex organs begin to grow to their normal adult size (a process that may take from two to five years), and their voices deepen. Boys experience erections, which occur during ninety per cent of their dreaming time. Nocturnal emissions begin to occur about once a month or oftener, usually starting one or two years after puberty begins. Beard growth begins several years after puberty, but both boys and girls grow pubic hair and underarm hair just before puberty. About one third of the boys have slight breast development during the time of puberty, but it soon disappears as the hormones become balanced.

Problems

These sudden changes produce several disturbing features for adolescents. First, the nose and hands seem to grow out of proportion. A boy wakes up one morning to find that he has a Roman nose (roamin' all over his face). His hands look like two big meathooks hanging at the end of long, skinny arms. Both boys and girls—especially early maturers—become somewhat awkward at this time; they seem to be always tripping over coffee tables and chair legs and spilling things in the cafeteria or at the dinner table. This period of awkwardness due to sudden growth usually lasts only a short time as they learn to adjust to changing body proportions.

A second problem with these changes is that most boys and girls have dreams of becoming a Mr. or Miss America. Boys in particular dream of becoming football heroes. Yet somehow their body image does not match this dream, for they are beginning to look very much like their mother or father. They are somewhat disappointed but must soon learn to accept their new body and appearance.

A third disturbing feature is that some girls and boys mature as early as ten years of age or as late as sixteen or seventeen. The average age for reaching puberty for girls is twelve and a half years, with some maturing as early as ten years and others maturing as late as sixteen years. Boys usually reach puberty about fourteen and a half years of age, with some boys maturing as early as eleven years and some as late as seventeen. Good nutrition, heredity, and stress are the main factors causing early maturity. For boys to mature early can be a distinct advantage: they can become athletic heroes since they are taller and heavier than most of the other boys in the sixth or seventh grade. Late-maturing boys have the problem of being smaller than the rest. However, for a girl to mature late is a distinct advantage to both her and the boys: she is smaller than the boys in her own grade and is not a threat to them.

Some boys and girls resent the changes that take place at puberty because they do not want to grow up. They want, like Peter Pan, to be children all their lives. They know that growing up means tremendous responsibility. However, the changes are inevitable; and one cannot stop the changes from taking place, although some girls try to stop them by going on strict diets and losing weight. It is God's desire that they become adult men and women to serve Him, and they must learn to be happy with the changes making them so. God has locked growth in their genes even before they were born (Psalm 139), and He knows exactly what changes will take place and when they will take place.

The physical changes bring about emotional ones. At twelve to thirteen years of age, girls begin to realize that boys do exist and are wonderful creatures. Of course, the objects of their attention are on the senior high level, and just about all of the boys in senior high school look very good to a junior high school girl. The boys in her grade will not mature for another two years.

Most junior high girls have had a crush on one or two unattainable persons who are either married or much too old for them, such as teachers, the coach, the preacher, the youth pastor, or the visiting evangelist. A crush usually lasts two or three weeks until they find a new object for their affection or until some senior high boy dates them.

When a boy is about fifteen years of age, he discovers that girls are very marvelous creatures and starts looking around for any girl who seems eligible. Usually he will look to junior high school girls who are on his same maturity level. This difference in maturity leads to the habit of dating girls somewhat younger.

Sometimes boys of junior high age make an about-face in behavior. If they have been model students, they may suddenly become mean and rebellious. This change is abetted by an upsetting home life in which Dad is often absent and Mother tries to maintain control of the family by screaming and yelling.

Solutions

Junior highers want to talk about these problems and other troubling incidents and situations. Mothers are often the ideal ones to talk to, for they have understood the son or daughter from infancy and are aware of the problems junior highers are going through. Some boys may find it more advantageous to talk to their fathers if the fathers are understanding. Sometimes the coach, the home economics teacher, the youth director, or the pastor can be a tremendous help by pointing out Bible principles to follow in solving these problems.

Parents can prepare pre-adolescents by informing and reassuring them about the physical and emotional changes to come. The age of ten or eleven is the best time for this preparation. In chapter five of his book *Hide or Seek,* James Dobson discusses the important ideas and attitudes that children need for the teen years. He also has tapes and a workbook on this subject which the children and their parents can use together.[1]

The most important principle for young people to remember is that God has His hand in all of the changes that are taking place. He knows all the problems and challenges they are facing. Trusting in the Lord in trying and difficult times and having a positive "praise the Lord" attitude about everything that happens will bring about peace and assurance. Acknowledging God and letting Him work in their lives (Proverbs 3:5-6) can help these junior high young people make these years the happiest years of their lives as they invest their energies in school and church involvement.

---

[1] These can be secured from Preparing for Adolescence, Pomona, CA 91768.

Chapter 5
The Senior High Years: Emerging Adults

In junior high school many boys and girls begin adolescence. But the wonderful adolescent time usually comes in high school for most young people. Adolescence is the time after puberty when the body has begun to mature into its adult form. It is a time of transition between childhood and adulthood. Adolescents are leaving the carefree, happy, do-as-you-please time of life when Mother and Dad make all the decisions, when their only responsibilities are making their beds and washing their hands before the evening meal, and when their only real concern is an older brother or sister who picks on them and always beats them at Monopoly. They are now facing the prospect of becoming adults with much graver responsibilities: choosing a vocation, finding the right boy or girl to marry, earning enough money to get married and support a family, having and raising children, voting, becoming a responsible citizen, and serving the Lord. They now must act upon the dedication decisions they may have made to become missionaries, preachers, Christian schoolteachers, or nurses. They must determine whether their faith and standards are based on Bible convictions or just convenience. They have new emotions and giant temptations about which they probably had never even thought when they were children.

Adjusting to Physical Changes

Adolescence can be the healthiest period of life; however, there are some physical problems connected with it. Teens can stay healthy if they eat a balanced diet, get proper rest, and get involved in physical activities, such as those available in their Christian high school and their youth group. However, fatigue is inevitable if they take on too many activities, fail to schedule their time properly, and stay up late at night to get everything done. It is important that they set goals, work out reasonable schedules, and refuse to procrastinate.

Being underweight or overweight can also be a problem, especially for girls. Some stubborn and manipulative girls who do not want to accept the responsibilities of adulthood go on extreme diets to lose a lot of weight and, as a result, damage their health. In severe cases girls become compulsive, developing anorexia nervosa. These need a doctor's help because the severe loss of weight stops their periods and reduces breast size, causing them to retreat to childhood, and can become severe enough to cause death. Teen-agers, of course, are naturally hungry most of the time, because they are using up a great deal of energy for activity and growth. Overeating, snacking, and too little activity can put them into an overweight pattern that is difficult to correct, especially if feelings of rejection are involved. These feelings must be dealt with before any diet can be successful.

Acne is another problem for many teen-agers. The cause for acne is not clear, but there seems to exist some relationship between acne and heredity, humid climates, and changing or unstable hormones during puberty. Many doctors are convinced that diet has little to do with acne. Adequate cleansing of the face is an important factor in controlling this problem. A daily cleansing routine with some special skin soap such as Neutrogena or another nonirritating soap is necessary. At times it is wise to let a good doctor or dermatologist prescribe medicine or treatment for the control of acne or the curing of infections that often follow the squeezing of these blemishes. Antibiotics may be prescribed by the doctor. Untreated infection may leave disfiguring scars that may then pose a self-concept problem. It is estimated that acne will disappear around age seventeen. Certainly, severe acne should not be ignored.

Posture can be another problem during the adolescent period, especially with girls who want to hide their breast development or try to make themselves look shorter than they really are. Sometimes, though, a medical problem with the back or spine needs to be diagnosed and treated by a doctor. Each teen-ager should be glad for the way God has made him, for God has his future in mind. A teen must learn the body-temple principle (I Corinthians 6:19-20), accepting his body as God has made him and praising Him for the wonderful way that He has worked in his life. He needs to realize that the physical changes have been ordained by Him so that the unique individual can be developed for His glory (Psalm 139).

Controlling Emotions

One of the most formidable tasks teens will have in the adolescent period is learning to control their emotions. Teenagers are typically moody. Studies have shown that both boys and girls tend to be on a fifteen-day cycle; they are euphoric for about ten to twelve days, then they have a three- to four-day period of depression, and then they are euphoric again. This cycle is the reason for their seeming emotional instability. Girls in particular tend to be emotionally upset just before their periods largely because of hormones which cause an accumulation of water in their body tissues. A girl can get into crying moods that cause her to run from the supper table at the least provocation. For boys, anger against Dad or Mom occurs as a result of the feeling of being overcontrolled.

Adolescent boys and girls want to be independent; as they become adults, they want to make their own decisions.

Parents, teachers, and youth workers should help teens make decisions on their own so that by the age of eighteen they can be fairly independent, only seeking guidance instead of requiring control. Getting the teen from the dependent childhood stage to the independent adult stage is a learning process for both the teen and the authorities over him. Teens should get more freedom to make decisions as they show maturity by following Bible principles in their daily lives.

In addition to moods, most teen-agers have certain fears, many of which are carried over from childhood. Especially they fear school-related or social situations that could cause embarrassment. They may fear having to recite something before the class, or they may fear saying something foolish on a date. They must learn to realize that these things happen to children, teen-agers, and adults alike and that crazy, stupid, upsetting incidents are very quickly forgotten by everyone involved. People soon forget even those highly embarrassing situations: times when a girl's skirt zipper breaks open or a boy faints in front of the class just before a speech. The best way to handle an embarrassing incident is to learn not to take oneself too seriously and to laugh at oneself along with the group.

Finding Identity

Finding identity is another task young people must accomplish in the senior high years. Accepting their masculinity or femininity is the first step to getting a proper identity. Boys need to develop muscle, learn how to work hard, keep a masculine haircut (I Corinthians 11:14), and achieve determined, manly gait and gestures. They must learn leadership and acquire a protective, gentle attitude toward women (I Peter 3:7). Girls must develop feminine characteristics and skills appropriate to women. Their hair styles, dress, and actions should never give a hint of masculinity. They should also become aware of the fragile male ego and how to avoid trampling on it and learn the art of yielding gracefully to a man's authority without feigning inferiority.

Teen-agers' second step in finding their identity is assessing their talents and abilities and using them to the glory of God. Instead of focusing on their weaknesses, they should concentrate on their strengths and how to develop them, praising God for the talents He has given them.

Third, they need to seek God and find what His purpose is for their lives (Proverbs 3:5-6). They should learn that God calls His servants to do what they can do, what they like to do, and what gives them peace. He also gives the power to do His will (Philippians 4:13; Ephesians 3:20).

The fourth step is learning to conquer rejection feelings that began at childhood and stem from the following four sources.

1. Negative and cruel things that others, including parents, older siblings, and elementary school friends have said about or done to them
2. Negative thoughts and statements they think and say about themselves, such as "I must be stupid for flunking that test" or "I must be weird to have done that."
3. Foolish comparison of themselves to others (II Corinthians 10:12)
4. Continuance in sinful habits that causes them to feel guilty and rejected by God

Charles Solomon has written two books, *The Rejection Syndrome* and *Handbook to Happiness,* dealing with the rejection feelings which hinder people from finding their identity. For the Christian, the only solution for rejection feelings is learning to live a crucified life (Galatians 2:20) and following the principle of Luke 9:23.

Sublimating Sexual Desire

A major problem for adolescents will be sexual desires that bring about many temptations. They must put the principle of purity into operation in their lives (I Thessalonians 4:1-7), learning to possess their bodies "in sanctification and honour." Boys have more problems with this temptation than girls; about ninety-five per cent of the boys have these strong desires in adolescence, whereas only about twenty per cent of the girls have these same desires. Girls' sexual desires develop very slowly, peaking when young ladies reach about twenty-five to thirty years of age.

Surveys show forty per cent of teen boys and twenty per cent of teen girls to be currently practicing the habit of masturbation. As a habit, masturbation is sinful because it is a self-centered act that can lead to lustful thinking, pornography, and illicit sexual behavior and later works against the normal marriage relationship of unity. The habit can be conquered by confessing it as sin, setting a goal for victory, and exercising regularly.

Sublimation of these sexual desires into work, study, sports, creative activity, and participation in a dynamic youth program is one way of handling these God-given desires. Letting God take care of desires through tension-releasing dreams, which girls also experience, is a second way of holding these desires under control until God brings the young person into contact with the man or woman of His choice for marriage and married love (Hebrews 13:4).

Teens who resist the temptations that are so common to man (I Corinthians 10:13) are those who make up their minds ahead of time to follow Bible principles as they act and react in various situations.

Dating

Dating is an area of great interest and potentially great problems in adolescence. A thousand and one questions come up about dating. The youth leader should have a series of messages explaining principles of dating that will give the teen-agers some helpful information. He should work with the parents in helping them to have some consistent answers and principles for their teens.

For example, group dating in the junior high school years and double dating in the high school years may be in order.

Since serious dating is the prelude to marriage, couples should date alone only in the years beyond high school. This is the time when parents should meet the potential boyfriend and give their approval before dating. Starting the date with prayer and ending the date with prayer and devotions can be a big step in making sure that the date is what it ought to be in glorifying the Lord. The following general rules give young people some guidelines for their conduct.

1. Never be alone in a house or in a parked car with your date.
2. Never do anything that you would not do if your mother or father were there with you.
3. Never date an unsaved person.
4. Always start your date with prayer.
5. Develop the art of good conversation by being well read and knowledgeable about current events and by being interested in the other person.
6. View every date as a potential mate, and refuse to date a person who does not meet Biblical standards.
7. Do not permit physical contact on a date (even kissing).

The purpose of dating in high school is to get to know as many girls and boys as possible. Young people are finding out what the opposite sex is like so that they can make the intelligent choice when the proper time comes. Going steady and becoming engaged during the high school years only thwarts the real purpose of high school dating.

Teens must learn to develop the art of conversation by asking appropriate questions; they also must learn all the little niceties and social graces that help make them the kind of social persons and partners that others want to date. Developing communication abilities will prepare them for future relationships as husbands or wives.

Resisting Peer Pressure

Finally, the biggest problem in adolescence is the desire to be like one's peers. If the teen leaders are doing certain things, such as getting involved with drugs, necking and petting, rebelling against authority, listening to rock music, smoking, drinking, or skipping classes or church meetings, other teens will have a strong desire to go along and be a part of the crowd. Insecure people will often do the "in" thing, whether it be in dress, activity, or attitude.

Teens need to learn to be independent, unique individuals, evaluating each situation and adjusting to the social group without sacrificing their own Bible standards. Learning to stand for the Lord and live by Bible convictions no matter what the crowd does is a mark of true character and will prepare the young person for the day when he will have to take a stand against compromise and Satan's infiltration in the church.

The separation principle (II Corinthians 6:14-18) is a tremendous help to teens in fighting Satan. Realizing the liberty that they have in Christ, they must learn to make decisions in line with Bible principles rather than to conform legalistically to someone's list of good and bad activities. They must learn to use this liberty to glorify God and not become a stumbling block to others (I Corinthians 8:9). Yet the youth group must set and maintain sound Biblical standards of conduct to give youth the boundaries needed to control the flesh from within and resist the devil and the world from without.

Parents should be the teens' greatest allies during the adolescent period; youth leaders must help parents understand teens and should encourage the parents to sit down with their teens every week for a listening and counseling time. Even though mothers are the confidantes for both sons and daughters through high school, fathers, too, need to take time with their children for fellowship and counseling. With the help of loving parents and a caring youth pastor, adolescents can not only survive but also enjoy the path to adulthood.

Chapter 6
Teaching Teens: Encouraging Discipleship and Service

A good youth leader should be able to teach as well as preach. A large part of his ministry involves solid teaching on everything from soulwinning to leadership.

Techniques

There are certain basic techniques that a teacher must follow in order to be successful.

Communicating principles

A great teacher teaches principles and not just facts. Facts are important because they buttress, illustrate, and illuminate the truth; but facts are the medium and not the message. Students tend to forget facts quickly, but principles become the hooks in the mind upon which to hang facts. Principles are the categories under which facts can be filed. Though facts help a learner to understand truth, it is principles that determine behavior. Therefore, the youth leader wants to help teens search out Bible principles in their devotions and apply them in daily life.

The teacher of teens is constantly pointing out the application of key Bible principles, for these build character. A person has character when he operates his life consistently on principle rather than feeling. God has told mankind plainly in His Word how to act and react in every situation. As Christians follow God's principles, they are promised success, happiness, and a full life (Joshua 1:8). Therefore, the youth leader trains his teens to ask in every situation, "God, what would You have me to do?" Even in trials, God promises good to those who love Him and follow His purpose (Romans 8:28).

Early in the history of the United States, Bible principles were constantly taught to children in the schools (which at that time were connected with churches and run by preachers). The early textbooks reflected this emphasis. The McGuffey Readers, written in 1837 by a Presbyterian preacher and his brother, were full of Bible principles. But around 1850 there was a secularization of education by Horace Mann, Henry Barnard, and other leading educators. The gospel and the Scripture were no longer the focal point of education; character traits and citizenship were emphasized instead. Revisions of the McGuffey Readers in 1857 and 1879 eradicated almost all of the references to Bible principles and salvation. During the first half of the twentieth century, Bible principles were practically eliminated in many of the churches under the influence of modernists and liberals, who also controlled Christian education in the Sunday schools and churches.

In 1954 Frank Gaebelein, in his book *The Pattern of God's Truth,* called for a revival of teaching of Bible principles in every academic subject. In 1963 Bill Gothard, then director of the Hi-C clubs in Chicago, started teaching ten foundational Bible principles which later developed into his Basic Youth Conflicts Seminar. (In 1984 he expanded these ten into two hundred Bible principles.) In 1965 Vera Hall and Rosalee Slater promoted the idea of principled teaching as the foundation for their Christian school curriculum. In 1972 the Bob Jones University School of Education developed thirty-seven Bible Action Truths, principles used in the Bob Jones University Press elementary Bible curriculum and in other elementary textbooks. (See Appendix A.) Dr. Ruth Haycock published a pamphlet in 1978 entitled "God's Truth in Every Subject," another listing of Bible principles in the academics. In 1984 she expanded this material into four volumes, and it was published by the Association of Christian Schools International.

This recently renewed emphasis on teaching and applying Bible principles is the heart of modern fundamentalist Christian education. It is the key to training youth "to be conformed to the image" of Christ (Romans 8:29), equipped to do "the work of the ministry" (Ephesians 4:12), and "throughly furnished unto all good works" (II Timothy 3:17).

As the teens study Scripture, the youth leader urges them to use the 4-M Formula (from Psalm 119:9, 11, 15, and 17): they should mark, memorize, meditate on, and master the principles that they find in their devotions. To train them to do this, he has Bible studies with them, perhaps covering the thirty-seven Bible Action Truths or Gothard's two hundred life principles. By learning these principles, teens gain not only daily guidance but also the knowledge of God's will for their lives.

Using illustrations

A superior teacher knows how to illustrate and simplify each truth that he presents. The purpose of illustration is to capture the attention of the listeners and to motivate them to accept the idea presented. A human-interest story, especially from the life of the youth leader, adds flavor and gives insights into the practical way that he himself follows Bible principles in his daily actions. Humorous sayings and jokes can add insight and capture interest too, but the teacher must keep them appropriate to the lesson and must avoid using the same ones over and over. (See Appendix L.)

Charts and diagrams are excellent ways of simplifying profound ideas. Clarence Larkin's book *Dispensational Truth* is full of charts, illustrations, and diagrams that make books of the Bible, such as Daniel and Revelation, easier to understand and that put the details of the Scripture into chronological perspective.

Dawson Trotman had unique ways of illustrating his ideas. He used the five fingers of the hand to represent the five steps of learning the Word: hear (Romans 10:17); read (Revelation 1:3); study (Acts 17:11); memorize (Psalm 119:9-11); and meditate (Psalm 1:2-3). He also used the fingers to teach the five kinds of prayer: confession, praise, thanksgiving, intercession, and petition. His unique wheel diagram showed Jesus Christ at the hub and the Christian life as the rim; the four spokes were prayer, witnessing, fellowship, and Bible study. And the seven stars of the Big Dipper were his essentials of Christian maturity: the gospel, follow-up, the hand, the wheel, setting the pace, reaching others, and worldwide vision. The north star, five hand-widths up from the front edge of the big dipper, represented Jesus Christ. Every time his students looked at the stars, a wheel, or their own hands, they were reminded of the points he was teaching.

Good Bible teachers have used all kinds of diagrams. With an overhead projector it is easy to present elaborate and colorful charts to a whole group with a minimum of expense. The following pages include descriptions of several diagrams along with the diagrams themselves (Tables II-V), which can be enlarged, photocopied, and transferred to a transparency for teaching.

The three-level diagram (Table II) can be used to illustrate the three positions of a person's relationship to God. The sin level is a diving board extended over a lake of fire. When a person reaches the age of accountability, he may fall off this precarious level into eternal fire at any time (die in his sins). He can get off this level by way of the cross elevator (receive Jesus Christ as Saviour) and get up on the spiritual level. To remain on this level (be constantly filled with the Spirit), he must confess his sins and live the crucified life (Luke 9:23). The moment he sins, he falls down to the carnal level. The carnal level may extend so far that it is hard to tell the unsaved sinner from the saved one. But the blessed-assurance barrier at the end of this level keeps him from sliding off (John 10:28-29). He can get back to the spiritual

Table II

Spiritual

Galatians 5:22-23

I John 1:9

Sin

Carnal

John 10:28-29

John 1:12

SIN

II Thessalonians
1:7-9

level by confessing his sins (I John 1:9). This diagram can be used in a series based on Romans 6-8, Galatians 2:20, and Romans 12:1-2. Soulwinning and discipling can also be taught using this diagram.

An effective diagram for senior high and college teens is the Love-Sex Desire diagram (Table III), used to present the purity principle (I Thessalonians 4:1-7). The chart is presented by first teaching the three phases of love (Part A of Table III). The first phase is the self-centered phase, from infancy to six years of age. For the first year and a half, the baby's love is centered on the mother; it then expands to include the father, relatives, playmates, and finally the first-grade teacher. During this period the parent is teaching the child to share with and care about others.

Around six years of age the child enters the second phase of love, that of the same sex. This is when boys have their best buddies and girls have their girlfriends. Those friendships should be encouraged, for both boys and girls are learning identification of their sex through their peers. This is an ideal time for fathers to befriend their sons and teach them masculine skills such as carpentry, mechanics, and lawn care; mothers should help their girls become feminine by teaching them cooking, sewing, and household duties.

At puberty (twelve years for girls and fourteen years for boys), the child switches to the third phase, love of the opposite sex, introduced by the junior high boy-crazy and girl-crazy stages. With maturity, the person settles down to dating, going steady with, becoming engaged to, and finally marrying one member of the opposite sex. If love is understood as an unselfish, self-sacrificing desire to meet the other person's needs, then marriage can become the ultimate in mature love.

The Sex Desire chart (Part B of Table III) can be overlaid on Part A. In the first stage (the first three years of life), the sex desire is zero; from three years to six years there is a slight rise in desire, called the exploratory phase. At this time boys and girls begin to play doctor and nurse with each other, and masturbation may start. Mother, though perhaps alarmed when she discovers these activities, should

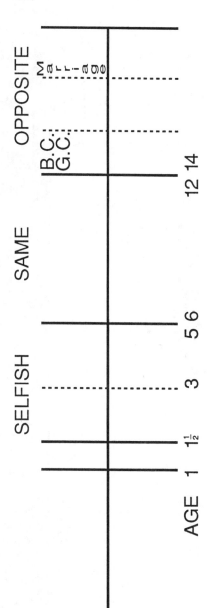

Table III-A

DEVELOPMENT OF LOVE

SELFISH   SAME   OPPOSITE

AGE 1 1½ 3 5 6 12 14

B.C.
G.C.

Marriage

Bob Jones University Press. Used with permission.

Table III-B

SEX DESIRE

GOD'S WAY | M | F

DEVIL'S WAY
SIN

M

Homosexual experience

Incest

Immorality
Immaturity

Sublimation
Dreams

Work
Sports
Study
Creative
Activities

M.L.
Heb.
13:4

Adultery

Fornication
Necking
Petting
PMS

Bob Jones University Press. Used with permission.

not overreact but simply tell her children that they are not to do these things. She can begin giving very basic sex education at this time.

The second stage, from six to puberty, is called the latency phase; sex desire is back at zero again. Now parents can help children set goals and begin to channel their energy into work, study, sports, and creative activities such as painting or practicing a musical instrument. It is important that boys associate with other boys and girls with other girls during this period, so that their sex identification is solidified.

In the third stage, starting at puberty, a boy's sexual desire (solid line) rises dramatically to its normal adult level. A girl's desire (dotted line) rises gradually to the age of twenty-five, when it reaches adult level. (About twenty per cent of the girls experience a sharp rise in sexual desire much like the male's and hence have the same problems that boys have controlling it.)

God's way of handling these desires is for teen-agers to sublimate them by channeling their energy into the activities begun in grade school. Men (and about twenty per cent of women) also experience tension-releasing dreams. God has provided marriage as the purpose for and outlet of sexual desire (I Corinthians 7:2; Hebrews 13:4). The purity principle of I Thessalonians 4:1-7 commands a Christian to maintain his sexuality in a blameless, God-honoring way. The devil, on the other hand, wants a person to express his sexuality through masturbation, necking and petting, premarital sex, adultery, incest, and in any other way that defies God's design.

The two charts together show that immorality is also immaturity. A woman who commits adultery not only has decided to be immoral but also is immature in her love development. She is still back in the boy-crazy stage of junior high. A man who has decided to be a homosexual is immoral and is still in the love-of-the-same-sex stage of late childhood. People are not locked into immorality, whether adultery or homosexuality, by overactive glands. They must decide to quit sinning, choose God's way of morality, and take steps to mature in their love development.

Table IV, for use with young high schoolers, illustrates the danger of necking and petting in dating relationships and the importance of setting limits on expressing affection until the wedding bridge can take them to the joys of married love.

The Mind Chart (Table V) is an excellent tool for teaching the proper use of the mind and the difference between positive faith thoughts and negative devil thoughts.

Besides graphic information, objects of all kinds can be used for illustrations and comparisons. A yardstick can represent a person's life, each inch of which equals two years. By scoring the yardstick at the three-, six-, nine-, eleven-, and thirty-inch marks (stages of life), the teacher can break off these sections of the yardstick as he talks about the finality of the passing of one's life, urging teens to make the present count for eternity.

Employing other methods

An outstanding teacher uses various techniques to get the students reacting mentally to the principles presented. Copies of the lesson outline with subpoints or key words missing can be distributed to the students so that they can follow the lesson by filling in notes as the teacher reveals the answers via overhead projector. Some youth leaders also urge the students to keep notes on all Bible messages that they hear.

Holding discussions helps students think about and evaluate what is being taught. As students respond verbally, they reveal their perception of the principles. The teacher then has opportunity to correct any misconceptions and false conclusions. Another method of eliciting student response is the anonymous survey/questionnaire (Appendices G and H-2). Having the students document their spiritual progress by filling out an annual testimony questionnaire helps both them and the teacher see how effective the youth group training has been. Observations of teens' behavior by parents and others also reveal to some extent the effectiveness of the teaching.

Table IV

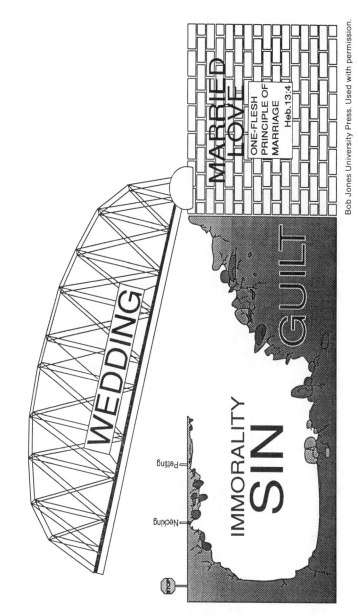

MARRIED LOVE

ONE-FLESH PRINCIPLE OF MARRIAGE

Heb. 13:4

WEDDING

GUILT

IMMORALITY SIN

Petting

Necking

Table V

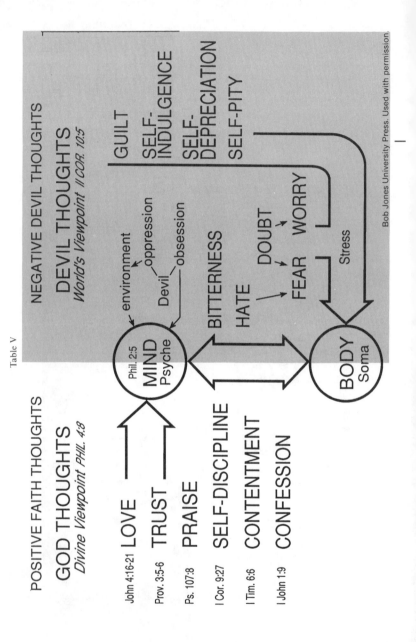

POSITIVE FAITH THOUGHTS

GOD THOUGHTS
Divine Viewpoint PHIL. 4:8

John 4:16-21 LOVE
Prov. 3:5-6 TRUST
Ps. 107:8 PRAISE
I Cor. 9:27 SELF-DISCIPLINE
I Tim. 6:6 CONTENTMENT
I John 1:9 CONFESSION

Phil. 2:5 **MIND** Psyche

BODY Soma

NEGATIVE DEVIL THOUGHTS

DEVIL THOUGHTS
World's Viewpoint II COR. 10:5

GUILT
SELF-INDULGENCE
SELF-DEPRECIATION
SELF-PITY

environment
oppression
Devil
obsession

BITTERNESS
HATE
DOUBT
FEAR WORRY

Stress

Bob Jones University Press. Used with permission.

A teaching tool that uses competition to create excitement is the quiz team. The youth group members are motivated to learn thoroughly whole books of the Bible upon which they will be questioned. A youth pastor would do well to put as much time, money, and effort into developing a quiz team as is used for sports teams. (Appendix B contains rules and strategy for fielding quiz teams.)

Showing enthusiasm

A motivating teacher is enthusiastic, able to inspire the students to love the subject that he is teaching. This enthusiasm is reflected not in wild gyrations and outlandish behavior but rather in the variation of intensity, pitch, and volume of the voice, as well as facial expression and open, definite gestures. Teens respond to this kind of excitement that a teacher shows for his subject. A positive, cheerful attitude with a touch of humor is also important to make teens want to learn.

A teacher with enthusiasm is somewhat of an actor, demonstrating to the teens how to put principles into action. With a stage area and a few simple props, he can act out the lessons taught in chart form. For example, in the three-level illustration (Table II), he can position himself on steps of the platform or in different chairs to picture the three different spiritual levels, talking through his lesson as he moves from place to place.

With a table the teacher can demonstrate the truth of I John 1:7-9. Sitting on top of the table (right with God), he has plenty of light to read his Bible; but when he gets under the table (backslides), the lack of light makes it hard to read his Bible (no communication with God). Confession of sin in this case does not change his position (salvation) but rather restores his condition (fellowship). This kind of enthusiastic, creative teaching helps teens to decide about and act upon the principles being taught.

Using positive reinforcement

A compassionate teacher uses positive reinforcement to build the teens' confidence in succeeding at learning and to foster their desire for further learning. Parents, teachers, and youth leaders are well acquainted with negative reinforcement: admonishing, rebuking, correcting, and punishing. Few use enough positive reinforcement in teaching their teens.

Positive reinforcement—the figurative pat on the back, the "word fitly spoken," the reward for a job well done, the public praise, the pictures and names of achievers posted on the church bulletin board—are all part of encouraging and not embarrassing teens in front of their peers. While teaching, the youth leader can nod, smile, or compliment a teen's answer to improve the reception of the material.

When asking questions, the compassionate teacher does not zero in on the sleepy student and embarrass him in front of the class by making him display his ignorance; rather, he generally addresses questions and lets the brighter students respond so that the whole group feels successful. A teacher shows real love when he helps his students to succeed.

Being Spirit-filled

A spiritual teacher must be filled with the Spirit if he is ever going to make an impact for God on the teens' lives. Confessed sins and a dedicated life are prerequisites for the youth leader who wants to see permanent positive changes in his students. Trusting in the power of the Holy Spirit to work in the hearts is the secret of effective Biblical teaching (Zechariah 4:6).

Material

What to teach to the teens is the big question for the youth leader who must prepare two to four messages a week. The following are some suggested areas to cover.

Doctrine of salvation

The youth leader must always teach a clear salvation message, for this is the heart of evangelism and one of the main purposes of the youth group. It must be plain and simple so that even the visitor with no Bible or church background can grasp the message. The Christian teens benefit from hearing the gospel reviewed with different illustrations and verses, for it gives them a fresh approach to their own soulwinning.

John 1:12 indicates that salvation is simply believing and receiving. First, one must believe the right things about Jesus Christ: that he is God, that He is the virgin-born Son of God, that He is sinless, that He shed His blood on the cross of Calvary as a payment for sins, that He was buried, that on the third day He arose from the dead, and that He ascended into heaven (I Corinthians 15:1-8; Mark 16). Without Jesus Christ and His shed blood on the cross as a payment for sin, there is no salvation.

Then a person receives Christ into his life to save him from the eternal judgment of his sins, trusting in Him and not in works, and repenting or turning from sin to Jesus Christ (Ephesians 2:8-9). This receiving involves a recognition of Him and Him alone as the Saviour from sin, realizing that having Jesus Christ in one's life is the only hope of heaven, and that accepting God's gift of eternal life is the final step for conversion (II Corinthians 13:5; Colossians 1:27; I John 5:11-13; Revelation 3:20). Without the personal contact with Jesus Christ, a person does not have salvation. Religion or man's works will not bring grace; it must be Jesus Christ plus nothing. In receiving Christ, the sinner repents or makes up his mind to turn from sin by choosing to go God's way rather than to continue going down the broad way that leads to destruction (Matthew 7:13). This changed life is proof that he has received Christ (II Corinthians 5:17).

Other topics

Besides the truth of salvation, there are certain topics pertinent to teens that should be covered at some time during their four years in the youth group. These ideas for lesson series, along with sources for materials, are given below, not necessarily in order of importance.

1. The seven decisions discussed in Chapter 2
2. The thirty-seven Bible Action Truths listed in Appendix A
3. Bill Gothard's two hundred life principles
4. Building character: Chapter 15 of *Formula for Family Unity* by Walter and Trudy Fremont; *The Disciplined Life* by Richard Taylor; *Character Sketches,* Volumes I-III, by Bill Gothard
5. Dispensations: *Dispensational Truth* by Clarence Larkin
6. Becoming a man or a woman: *The Disciplined Life* by Richard S. Taylor; *Beauty and the Best* by Beneth Jones
7. Male-female relationships: *Quality Friendship* by Gary Inrig; *Dating* by Scott Kirby
8. Basic ideas on marriage: *Formula for Family Unity; The Christian Family* by Larry Christianson
9. Career opportunities in full-time Christian service, including a survey of the colleges and universities that train for these positions: college catalogs
10. Leadership: *Spiritual Leadership* by Oswald J. Sanders; *Management for the Christian Leader* by Olan Hendrix; *Be the Leader You Were Meant to Be* by Leroy Elms
11. Music: *Can Rock Music Be Sacred?* and *The Big Beat: A Rock Blast* by Frank Garlock; the Symphony of Life cassette series from Majesty Music, Inc.
12. Holy living: *The Pursuit of Holiness* and *The Practice of Holiness* by Jerry Bridges; *Ancient Landmarks* by Frank Hamrick
13. Adjustments: *Your Reactions Are Showing* by Alan J. Peterson; Chapter 11 of this book lists twelve adjustments that teens must make for future happiness

14. Finances: Larry Burkett's personal finance seminars
15. The Spirit-flesh model: *Handbook to Happiness* by Charles Solomon; Table IX and Chapter 11 of this book

Decisions

Teens who are still faithful full-time servants of God twenty years later have made a number of decisions for the Lord along the way. In addition to the seven listed in point 1 above, the decisions may include having devotions, not working on Sunday, passing out tracts, memorizing Scripture, limiting TV viewing, getting rid of sinful habits, having a balanced emphasis on sports, obeying authority, setting goals, correcting a poor diet, and having a positive faith attitude.

The youth leader in his teaching aims for decisions, constantly urging the teens to make choices and to make up their minds. These decisions do not have to be the down-the-aisle type to be genuine, but the teens should be challenged to make definite vows before God and to record them in their Bibles. They can make their commitment public by raising a hand, throwing a stick on the campfire, or even by telling a best friend, a parent, or the youth leader. Real learning has taken place when a person changes his behavior because of it, putting into practice the command of James 1:22.

In monthly parents' meetings, the youth leader lets the parents know what he is teaching by capsulating the lessons and distributing copies of the outlines. Parents can then strengthen that teaching in their family devotions. The parents and the youth leader are on same side, supporting each other's ministries and striving for the same decisions and changes in their teens.

Principle-based, illustrated, enthusiastic, positive, Spirit-filled teaching can indeed build a strong youth group, change lives, and prepare full-time servants of God.

Chapter 7
Activities:
Ideas for an Exciting
and Dynamic Program

Activities are the initial motivating factor to get teens excited and involved in the youth program. In addition, appropriate activities can be a potent force in attracting unsaved teens to attend the group's gospel presentations, one of the primary purposes for having activities. Certain activities such as gospel teams, quiz contests, and talent nights can become a teaching tool and an avenue toward full-time service.

Elements

A few general principles for planned activities follow.

Fun and excitement

Fun activities should be wholesome, challenging, exciting, novel, and adrenaline producing. Teens get tired of the humdrum, fly-buzzing monotony of life at home and at school. They are looking for something socially exciting to appear on the horizon of the week or month to highlight it and make it significant. Competition enhances the fun and stirs up enthusiasm. Everyone should participate on the teams, which should be divided as evenly as possible. A classification of these activities for fun is given in Table VI.[1]

Exciting, scary, difficult, and challenging activities like water or snow skiing, parasailing several hundred feet in the air over a lake, going down a 300-foot superslide, mountain climbing, and horseback riding get teens' dynamic energies sublimated, channeled, and released in wholesome ways. If they are screaming and breathless occasionally, the teens will come back for more.

Participation

Teens have enough spectator activity in television viewing and high school sports. Activities should require participation. When putting on a skit, the youth leader should get as many teens involved as possible. When using group activities such as capture the flag with its variations, everyone should be part of a team, and the lay leaders should be the jailers. The teens should help in the planning and execution of the big activities. They should be on the committees, buying and cooking the food at the big steak fry, writing the hilarious script for the annual banquet program, or planning and running the Special Olympics program. The youth leader will be amazed at the creative productions and hidden talent that spring forth. (He must be ready to give guidance when creativity goes to extremes.) Teens will attend and get others to attend the activities that they themselves have planned and are presenting.

Evangelism

An activity should include not only a devotional but also a regular gospel presentation with an invitation. Teens should be using the social activities as a point of contact and an opportunity to invite their unsaved friends to have a good time, with the ultimate purpose of winning those friends to Christ. Most teens feel very lonely and outside the social group. The Christian teen should be well aware of the "M&M" (Mix and Mingle) and "D&C" (Divide and Conquer) principles. Instead of buddying up with his old school friends, the Christian teen should meet the visiting teens and make them feel right at home and accepted. He should separate one of the visitors from the security of his gang or best friend and become a new friend to him. He should be with the visitor when he makes his decision for Christ and then should meet with him at least once a week for follow-up and discipleship.

Refreshments

The food at an activity can be simple fare: something solid (sandwiches, hamburgers, brownies), something salty (potato chips, corn chips, or cheese curls), and something to wash it down (pop, Kool-Aid, or fruit juice). (See Appendix C.) Food should be served after the fun and games and just before the singing and message. A few chords on the piano make a smooth transition from the eating to the singing, which is followed by the message. These phases can be held in the same room with the teens sitting on the floor, if necessary. If a move is made to another room or building, a part of the crowd will be lost.

Flexibility

Imagination and flexibility are the two vital characteristics of a good youth leader in arranging activities. He can take just about any activity and adapt it to his group and situation. One youth leader substituted an indoor track and field Olympics for the outdoor one thwarted by week-long rain. He used paper plates for the discus throw, cotton balls for the shot-put, straws for the javelin throw, feet tied together for relay races, and so on. Once the objective is determined, an activity can be adapted in any way necessary to fit the situation, talents, and group.

Safety

Calling parents to tell them of an accident or tragedy involving their teen would be doubly hard if the leader knew that he had not taken every measure to prevent the problem or minimize its severity. A good first-aid kit with Adrenalin and splints (see Appendix D) and a trained first-aid worker with CPR knowledge are essential. A lifeguard should be present for any water activity. Having such training himself enhances the usefulness of the youth leader, especially in a small youth group.

A 40-foot nylon rope and a folded 6 mm plastic sheet, 12 × 24 feet, can be handy on hikes. Blankets, sweaters, and extra jackets should be available in situations where hypothermia might be a problem. For example, on Mount Washington in New Hampshire, the temperature can drop forty degrees in one hour. Add to that 40-50 mile-per-hour winds, and there is a real wind-chill problem. Getting the group off the mountain and into a sheltered place would be imperative. Getting the group off the water and out of open spots in an electrical storm or in gale-force winds can be a problem if the leader is not aware of coming weather conditions or the peculiar weather characteristics of an area. In very hot areas in the South or West, where temperatures range above 90° F, a leader must be aware of heat exhaustion, heat stroke, and dehydration. The group should be kept out of the sun between noon and two o'clock. Salt pills and plenty of liquids should be available, and sweaty activities should not be scheduled for longer than two hours.

Cars and buses used in transportation should have CB radios; walkie-talkies for the leaders can be helpful in keeping track of a large group. Each leader should have the emergency numbers for the areas where the group will visit so that help can be contacted quickly.

Glory to God

The holiness of God influences the type of activity and the manner in which it is conducted. The godly youth leader does not have a mixed beach or pool party or take the teens to a rock concert. The trips, retreats, and camps are well chaperoned and give attention to modesty and the care of the body, including cleanliness, nutrition, exercise, and sleep. The leader's discipline controls outlandish and offensive behavior that would mar the testimony of the group. Evangelism is always emphasized, and the success of the activity is gauged by the degree to which the goals of salvation and edification are reached.

Ideas

For ready reference, the youth leader should have a list of all possible places of activity within a 300-mile radius of the church. The list should include telephone numbers of the managers, prices, special group rates, and times of opening and closing. Local maps and brochures should be a part of this file. It should also include names of possible speakers and appropriate films. Having information from travel agencies can also be helpful, and every time the leader goes on vacation or visits his relatives for Thanksgiving or Christmas, he should be collecting brochures and details of places along the way. All this information should be on hand at the planning session, for the session is most effective if someone can call right then and make the reservation, contact the speaker, or reserve the film.

The youth leader should plan about one big social activity a month and go all out with publicity, promoting it as a successful, exciting, and evangelistic attendance booster that will win the unsaved, edify the Christians, and build the youth group. A list of kinds of activities that a youth leader can use anytime during the year is given at the end of Chapter 2. A list of possible social activities for specific times of the year follows:

January—Snow skiing, ice-skating, tobogganing, or roller-skating

February—Parent-appreciation, valentine, or sweetheart banquet

March—Bowling

April—Easter sunrise service and breakfast

May—Junior-senior banquet (the younger teens serve the meal and present the program)

June—Deep-sea fishing, white-water rafting, or super-spectacular trip

July—All-day hike; retreat program with water activities such as skiing, parasailing, boat races, etc.

August—Camp

September—"Grand ol' Uproar" program at a farm

October—Horseback riding and a cookout
November—Progressive supper or party
December—Caroling at malls, hospitals, or senior citizens
    homes with a party following the singing

Large-scale activities

A super spectacular trip should be planned once a year.
(See list in Table VII for ideas.) The best places to go will
be determined by the part of the country where the group
is based. A comfortable bus could be chartered if the church
doesn't own one, but bus trips of more than three thousand
miles round-trip can be disasters. On occasion, special bargain
flights to a hub city can be secured, and a bus can be rented
there for the trip to the nearby attraction. Camping overnight
in sleeping bags, singing, activities on the bus, and short
stopovers for sightseeing can make long bus trips less boring.

These trips should combine evangelism and missionary
effort with sightseeing, adventure, and fun. Adventures that
introduce the teens to God's great creation include hiking
to the bottom of a canyon, having a campfire service on
top of a mountain, canoeing in the Canadian or Wyoming
wilds, or white-water rafting. June seems to be the best month
for these trips; highways and accommodations are not too
crowded, and the trips won't interfere with the main family
vacation months of July and August. (Table VIII details
procedures for a Grand Canyon trip.)

Small-scale activities

Below are some explanations and suggestions for the
activities listed in Table VI.

Bike or car rallies may be organized that take the teens
to various stops as they follow clues. The first group to
complete the course wins. At the intermediate stops where
the groups get further instructions, they can have refreshments
or a particular activity, such as a game or a skit.

Treasure hunts are similar to bike or car rallies in that
teens follow clues from place to place to the location of the

hidden treasure. The clues and the prizes may be keyed to a theme, if desired. There should be as many sets of clues as there are groups, and the clues should be hidden in reverse order so that the description of the hiding places is as accurate as possible. The three or four hidden treasures can be paperback books or things to eat (either coupons to be redeemed at a restaurant or actual food items, such as fruit or candy). The length of the route on the treasure hunt should not be more than two to four miles so that the teens can walk; they should follow a circular route so that they end up near the starting point, and they will not have a four-mile walk back after it is over.

Scavenger hunts are designed to collect a list of objects—autographs, sounds, ingredients for a pizza, pictures, or even teen-agers. The leader should never have the groups do or get any of the following items.

1. Anything illegal (such as a section of the courthouse fence)
2. Anything they have to take back (a tricycle, or a truck tire and rim)
3. Anything that will put them in the place of temptation or hurt their testimony (an empty beer bottle)

A typical list of objects might include the following items.

five olives	a coin minted in the birth
a fresh egg	year of someone in the
a live frog	group
a dust ball from under a	an old license plate
bed	an old negative
an oak leaf	a Polaroid picture of the
a pancake	collecting team
a piece of rusty barbed wire	a seashell
a boiled egg	a marble
a two-week-old newspaper	

The collected items can then be incorporated into a culminating activity, e.g., holding a frog-jumping contest with the collected frogs. If it is raining, have an indoor hunt right in the meeting room. The teens can get objects in the room or on their person, such as a slip-on shoe, a piece of toenail, a black hair, two belts, etc.

Water sports will vary with the body of water and the facilities and equipment available. Swimming, surfing, water skiing, boating (cruise boats, sailboats, power boats, canoe, and rowboats), tubing, parasailing, fishing, watermobiling, and supersliding all use water as the primary agent for fun. Inexpensive means of fun can be rigged up, such as a trolley ride across the lake or a rope hanging from a tree to swing the teen from the hillside out over the lake. Competition enlivens water activities, and water polo, basketball, volleyball, or races can discharge a lot of energy. Modesty is in order for these activities, and some of the activities might require segregation of the sexes to maintain the standards of the group.

Snow sports can have a tremendous appeal if the group resides in the snow belt or in a mountainous area. Ski resorts in states such as North Carolina, Tennessee, and northern Georgia are now active in January and February. These resorts offer fairly inexpensive group rates for lift tickets and equipment rental. The youth leader should call ahead about snow conditions and temperature before making the trip.

In snow-belt states many of the youth have their own skis, toboggans, ice skates, and sleds, and fleets of snowmobiles are usually available. Using truck inner tubes for tubing down hills or flooding the athletic field for ice-skating makes for fantastic, inexpensive fun. A warm cabin or lodge with restrooms should be available for meals and a comfortable meeting after the fun.

Farm activities require a farm, a big barn, and an owner that likes teens. A "Grand Ol' Uproar" or a "Flea-Haw" can be staged with guitars, banjos, and singing for fun. The activities can include milking a cow, catching a greased pig, and having a mud hole fight. Contests might include a corn-kernel throw, a rope climb, and a rope-swinging relay. These activities could be correlated with a hayride from the church to the farm. The hay wagons must be well-lighted for safety, and cars in front and behind the caravan of wagons are necessary, especially in hill country. A pig, steer, or chicken barbecue completes the activity, if there is a willing barbecue cook (with the equipment) in the church.

Outdoor activities are designed to get teens in touch with God's creation, enjoying the beauties and solitude of the woods and mountains and sky that God has made. Hiking to special nature sites (the top of a mountain, a cliff, a land formation, or a historical site) will depend on what is available in your area. These hikes are best done in the spring when the trees are blooming or in the fall as the leaves are changing color.

Eating is usually a part of these activities. Barbecues, hamburger or steak fries, and hot dog and marshmallow roasts are extra special out in the woods or on the beach.

Orienteering is a relatively new competition in the woods, and it is becoming popular in certain areas.[2] Also popular are field days with cross-country running and outdoor games such as capture the flag.

Parent-teen activities, with competition, are designed to bring father and son and mother and daughter together. Ball games, swimming, boating, fishing, retreats, camp outs, family camps, and other activities that parents and teens enjoy can be scheduled. In competitions family members should be put on the same side to increase family cooperation and unity. Being together for the same spiritual experience is an important step for a family as the teens and their parents are challenged by the messages, testimonies, singing, invitation, and campfire service. (This need for family unity is one reason that having a separate teen-age section in church is not always the best policy. The aim is to increase family unity, not fracture it. Any teen whose parents do not attend should be in a special teen section in the front.)

Parties are big hits with most teens. Holidays are natural party times. The Christmas party could follow a carol sing in the malls. The gift exchange could be enhanced by having everyone bring a wrapped gift not costing over a dollar, putting the gifts in a big pile, and choosing the recipients in numbered order. Being able to make a demand trade of gifts with one another before the gift is opened adds excitement to the exchange. The person receiving the unopened exchange gift can demand an exchange from someone else. No gift can be exchanged more than three times. The games and program must be carefully planned ahead.

Progressive parties and suppers ideally cover a circular route with about eight homes involved. One song, one short game, and one thing to eat is scheduled at each home. If the circuit can be made on foot, having the group of teens sing as they walk down the suburban street is good publicity for the church, and other teens may be invited to join the group as they go. Dessert, message, and invitation are at the last house, which should be near the starting point where all the cars are parked. Ten to twenty minutes at each house and five minutes for travel for a total of two hours is about right to keep the activity moving.

Silly competition supplies hilarious fun, good publicity, and sometimes a new statistic for the record book. Two youth groups in a certain town reserved a center area in a mall for a week-long marathon volleyball game. Any teen could sign up to play for any length of time. They got the names, addresses, church affiliation, and answers to other survey questions (such as their view of how to get to heaven) from over one thousand teens who played in the game. These were witnessed to and later followed up. The record (186 hours) for the Guiness book of records stood for at least a month, and the group got sports-page publicity and even some television coverage one evening.

Bathtub, Volkswagen, or phone booth stuffing can include rules like requiring at least four parts of the body to be within the object to be stuffed and no part of the body touching the ground outside the object. Again, as with water sports, church standards concerning separate boy-girl competition need to be upheld.

Organization

In planning activities, the leader needs to supervise the following areas and, if possible, get a teen committee with a lay leader working on each area.

1. Food
2. Facilities
3. Program, including music and speaker
4. Games and equipment
5. Transportation
6. Publicity

The publicity should include the time, the type of dress, the costs, what to bring, the mode of transportation, and directions to the event. Enough copies should be made to have four for each teen—one to keep and three to pass out to the friends he is going to invite—and should be given to the teens four weeks prior to the activity. The youth leader should plan about twelve main social activities a year, and give each at least four weeks' publicity in order to have a good turnout.

Teens are very peer oriented; they want to go where other teens are. This desire should be used to the group's advantage. The teens should sign up at the youth meeting if they have the slightest idea that they can attend. A "paid" column should be drawn on the right-hand side of the list, and their money should be collected the following week. The leaders' names should already be at the top of the list before the list is passed around (teens tend to follow the leaders). Most of the teens will sign up, and most will pay. As other teens see the big list that is posted, they will want to get in on a good thing and even get their friends signed up. For camps and retreats, a down payment must be secured. Teens rarely back out if they have put some money down.

Activities, if planned and run properly with the right objectives in mind, can be a tremendous help in developing a strong, dynamic, growing youth group.

---

[1] THE WILDS, Box 796, Taylors, SC 29687, publishes S.O.A.P. Publications. These volumes contain detailed ideas of all sorts of fun activities. Every youth leader should get his church to purchase the whole set of these books as ready reference when the teens are planning the year's activities and the monthly events.

[2] Further information can be ordered by mail from the American Orienteering Service, 308 West Fillmore, Colorado Springs, CO 80907.

Table VI

Activities for Fun

A. Bike/car rallies
B. Treasure hunts
C. Scavenger hunts
    1. Regular list of objects
    2. Autographs
    3. Pennies that multiply—bigger and better
    4. Tape recordings (e.g., the moo of a cow)
    5. Polaroid pictures (e.g., a living pyramid with a fire truck in background)
D. Water sports (dress standards set ahead by pastor and deacons)
    1. Skiing; parasailing
    2. Swimming; snorkling; skin diving
    3. Boating and fishing; deep-sea fishing trips; white-water rafting; tubing
E. Snow sports
    1. Skiing
    2. Ice-skating; sailing
    3. Tobogganing; tubing; snowmobiling
F. Farm activities
    1. Greased pig in muddy field; mud wrestling
    2. Milking cows
    3. Barn program
G. Outdoor events
    1. Ice-cream social; the town's longest sundae
    2. Hamburger or steak cookout

3. Barbecue: whole steer or pig, ribs, chicken
4. Field day
5. Orienteering (*Reader's Digest,* February 1975, p. 119)
   American Orienteering Service
   308 West Fillmore
   Colorado Springs, CO 80907
6. Hikes
7. Biking or horseback riding

H. Parent-teen activities
   1. Campouts and cookouts
   2. Suppers: bean, pizza, soup, spaghetti
   3. Banquets
   4. Teas for girls and their mothers
   5. Father-son and mother-daughter sports competition
   6. Biking
   7. Skating

I. Parties
   1. Skating: roller and ice
   2. Holiday: Christmas, Valentine, etc.
   3. Birthday and theme

J. Silly competitions
   1. Stuffing a bathtub
   2. Packing a bus
   3. Eating what's in the bag
   4. Eating with no hands: pie, watermelon, sundae, etc.
   5. Running marathons

Table VII
Super Spectacular Trips

1. Do not take teams or groups from school for more than three or four days or from their families on traditional family holidays, such as Christmas, Easter, or Thanksgiving.
2. Plan about one year in advance for the most inexpensive and best reservations. Teens must know the approximate cost if they are to earn and save the money for the trip. Your own part-time job placement agency may develop out of this.
3. Take the trip yourself beforehand, perhaps as a vacation. This advance planning gives you an opportunity to reconnoiter and find out the best and most worthwhile experiences for your teens. It is also a good time to check accommodations and prices. Your travel agent can be a big help here for group rates, campgrounds, best travel arrangements, etc. Be aware of airline bargains. Do as much cooking out and camping out as possible to save money. Use churches and camps for sleeping and church gyms and houses for hot meals and showers.
4. See and do as many things as possible in the given area and on the way there and back. Take a circular route if possible so that you are not going over old ground. Deep-sea fishing, mountain climbing, sightseeing at historical places, attending cultural activities, and having other experiences are all a part of learning.

5. Have a continual gospel thrust: pass out tracts; witness; conduct Bible studies on the bus; have gospel teams performing in street meetings, jails, missions, churches, beaches, and shopping centers. Make a missionary trip out of it.

6. Prepare for emergencies: take along a complete first-aid kit; splints; a person with first-aid training; extra blankets, towels, sheets, and jackets. Give the young people a list of things they should pack. Always think of safety and the best possible comfort.

Suggestions for Trips

1. Alaska—up the Alaskan Highway
2. Arizona—Grand Canyon (South Rim), Bryce Canyon, Zion National Park, and Hoover Dam
3. California—Yosemite National Park, Catalina Island, San Diego Naval Base, San Francisco, Muir Woods, Lucerne, Sequoia Forest, and the seacoast
4. Colorado—Steamboat Springs, Aspen, Leadville, Cripple Creek Gold Mine and road to Colorado Springs, Garden of the Gods, Pike's Peak, Cave of the Winds, Air Force Academy, Rolling Valley Ranch, Casa Bonita Restaurant in Denver, Rocky Mountain Park near Boulder, and Mt. Evans in Golden
5. Connecticut—Mystic Sea Village
6. Florida—Okeefenokee Swamp, Florida Keys, Kennedy Space Center, Disney World
7. Georgia—Stone Mountain, Six Flags in Atlanta
8. Louisiana—New Orleans, Mississippi Delta
9. Massachusetts—Plymouth Rock, Cape Cod
10. Michigan—Detroit, Dearborn Village and Museum, Mackinac Straits and Island
11. New Hampshire—White Mountains and Mt. Washington
12. New York—New York City, Schroon Lake, Ticonderoga
13. North Carolina—The Wilds, Biltmore House and Farm, Outer Banks, Kitty Hawk, Light House, Coast Guard

station, ferry ride, shrimp packing plant, the Moravian Village at Winston-Salem
14. Pennsylvania—Philadelphia
15. South Carolina—Bob Jones University, Charleston
16. Tennessee—Great Smoky Mountains (part is in North Carolina), Oak Ridge, Norris Dam
17. Utah and Wyoming—Salt Lake City, Yellowstone National Park, Bear Tooth Pass, and Cody
18. Virginia—Georgetown, Williamsburg, Jamestown
19. Washington—Olympia National Park, Grand Coulee Dam
20. Washington, D.C.
21. Canada—Montreal, Quebec, Vancouver, Victoria, Banff, Lake Louise, and Ice Fields in Jasper National Park
22. Canada and United States—Niagara Falls, Thousand Islands, St. Lawrence Seaway
23. Caribbean—Puerto Rico—Old San Juan, the rain forests, ferry ride from Fahardo to St. Thomas (Stay at the U.S. federal campground on St. John's Island for ideal snorkling. Equipment is available for rent at several beaches, especially Trunk Bay.)
24. Mexico—Tijuana, Mexico City, and the pyramids

Travel agent services are free, and they can save you money with special fares, rates, and package deals. Contact Unusual Tours, Bob Jones University, Greenville, South Carolina 29614. Phone: (803) 271-3338.

Table VIII
A Super Spectacular Trip: Grand Canyon-South Rim

Make reservations with a travel agent eight months in advance. June is a good month for this trip.

1. Register at Bright Angel Lodge. Pick up Phantom Ranch reservations. Each person should have two quarts of water, fruit, slacks, long-sleeved white shirt, small knapsack, and crushable hat with brim.

2. Have someone take you to Yaki Point (five miles from Bright Angel Lodge), or take the bus. This is the starting point for Kaibob Trail—down 7.5 miles. Stop every half hour to rest and drink water. Time: 3-5 hours.

3. Stay at Phantom Ranch or camp out. A night's lodging in air-conditioned dorms and three meals (supper, breakfast at 5:00 A.M., and a sack lunch) cost about $35.00. You can buy fruit, snacks, and drinks at the canteen at Phantom Ranch.

4. For a beautiful canyon sightseeing tour while at Phantom Ranch, hike up and back in the early evening on the North Rim Trail, about 1-2 miles past the two bridges. Phantom Canyon is on your left past the second bridge.

5. Get up the next morning at 4:30 and have breakfast at 5:00. Start up the Bright Angel Trail by 5:15 (9.5 miles, 5-7 hours). Indian Gardens is 5 miles from the bottom; water and shade are available. From there take a side hike of 3 miles round trip for spectacular view of the

plateau point. The last 4.5 miles to the South Rim is from 6,000 to 7,000 feet. Stop and rest every 15 minutes. Depth of canyon to river is 5,000 feet, or about 1 mile.

6. Take the East Rim Drive (U.S. 64) and stop at all overlook points, ending at Desert View Point.

7. Take Route 64 to Cameron and go on to Bryce Canyon. At Sunset Point in Bryce Canyon hike down to the bottom on the 1.5-mile round-trip trail, or take one of the longer trails.

8. Take Route 89 down to Route 12, and take Route 12 through Zion National Park.

9. In Zion National Park drive up the 12-mile canyon and picnic at the end.

10. The Hoover Dam tour takes one hour and leaves every 15 minutes between 8:00 and 5:00. A film about the dam can be seen in Boulder City the night before the tour.

11. The circle from Phoenix, Arizona, and back is 1,100 miles. If you leave from Phoenix to go to the South Rim of the Grand Canyon, go up beautiful Oak Creek Canyon on Alternate 89 just below Flagstaff. There are about 26 miles of magnificent views.

For Phantom Ranch reservations or hotel reservations, write to the following address:

Reservations Department
Grand Canyon National Park Lodge
Grand Canyon, Arizona 86023
Phone: (602) 638-2401

Chapter 8
The Camping Ministry: Roughing It with Results

A unique tool of the youth leader for evangelizing and edifying teens is camping, and a good youth program will provide camping experiences for all the youth. Camps have played a significant part in many Christians' lives. Surveys taken by national youth organizations and in psychology classes at Bob Jones University indicate that about thirty per cent of the salvation or dedication decisions that teens make are made at a camp.

Advantages

The advantages of camping are threefold: the concentrated gospel emphasis, the wholesome Christian environment, and the contact with God's great creation.

The typical weekend retreat may offer as many as five or six messages, a film, and discussion groups, while the week-long camp may include as many as fifteen to eighteen messages. In addition, there are usually cabin devotions and a quiet time when the camper gets alone with God in prayer and Bible study. One week of camp actually equals a nightly attendance at a two-week revival. This concentrated gospel emphasis sets up an atmosphere in which the Holy Spirit can bring conviction and confront the camper with the decisions of faith he needs to make.

At camp, teens are in a separated Christian environment away from the peer pressure of their friends, rock music, conflict at home, and electronic devices such as TV and stereo. In the camp environment, counselors can deal individually with the campers' problems, give them direction, and follow up with Bible principles and exemplary behavior. The sports, games, programs, and hilarious fun, which cannot be duplicated back home, make the camp an enjoyable but purposeful time for the teens.

Another advantage is that camping reveals to teens the greatness of God's unchanging, stable creation. The North Star, the Big Dipper, and other constellations are in the same proximity to one another as they were in the past and as they will be in the future. The croak of a frog, the coo of the mourning dove, and the hoot of the owl are unchanging. Even the seasons with their changes are constant year after year, and all of God's creation is a manifestation of His stability and permanence, pointing the camper to eternal things in Christ.

A good camp will make available an organized nature study so that the camper can get a taste of God's great power and majesty. Nature classes, hikes along a well-titled nature trail, a study of the stars with a telescope, observations of animals and birds, and rugged wilderness trips put the camper into direct contact with nature and point out the necessity of learning skills to cope with the natural environment. A teen who learns to relate to God's creation gains experience in handling himself in many other situations.

Types

A Christian camp or retreat usually involves one or more nights away from home in the woods or in an isolated place for the purpose of evangelizing and edifying its participants. Camps and retreats can vary in nature, from permanent, organized camps to church-sponsored weekend retreats, week-long camps, or camping trips. The activities at these camps often include water sports, hiking, mountain climbing, horseback riding, and other activities that cannot usually be experienced at home or at school. The weekend retreat is a popular camp, for teens are out of school and adults are free to help.

A camp can be platform-centered, counselor-centered, program-centered, or a blend of all three. The platform-centered camp is patterned after the old camp meetings that brought families to a campground to hear good preaching. The ones from far away would camp out overnight or stay in cabins on the grounds. It was a revival in the woods with facilities provided. Many groups in the late 1800s and early 1900s used the old "Chatauqua" grounds for their facilities. Platform-centered camps are characterized by five or six preaching meetings or classes per day and are frequently called camp meetings.

The idea for a counselor-centered camp was developed in the early 1900s mainly by liberals who objected to all the preaching. They believed that the gospel was best communicated by a life, and the one-on-one method was the way to reach youth in camp. Indeed, this method can be an effective way of influencing the camper if the counselors are trained, if they work all summer during every week of camp, and if the counselor-camper ratio isn't too high (1:10 maximum). The program is usually loosely structured, allowing plenty of free time for the camper to talk with his counselor and contemplate the things that he is learning. Usually no more than one preaching service a day is held.

The program-centered camp, on the other hand, is geared around a fast-paced program that keeps the campers busy throughout the day. Successful program camps have been based on all the following:

1. A horse ranch providing trail rides, rodeos, and training in riding and caring for horses
2. Competition in unusual sports not experienced at home
3. Water activities of all kinds
4. Hiking and mountain climbing, focusing on exploring nature
5. Training for a major sport

6. Music, emphasizing both vocal and instrumental competition and training
7. Drama and entertainment
8. Computer training

Most camps have two or more of these programs going on at one time. The program is used to attract youth and to give them something different to do; but the gospel, the real purpose of the camp, is presented in meetings, counselor contact, and devotional times.

The best camps combine all three approaches. A good example is the Wilds Christian Camp and Conference Centers in North Carolina and Colorado. They have at least three preaching or teaching classes a day, trained counselors who work with seven to nine campers a week, and unique programs combining competition, water activities, hiking and nature study (including an observatory), horses, and hilarious entertainment. The Bill Rice Ranch in Tennessee, Camp Joy in Wisconsin, Camp Co-Be-Ac in Michigan, Camp Ironwood in California, and many others specialize in unique approaches to Christian camping. There are also many denominational camps throughout the country that have been used to reach thousands of teens through the years.

Preparation

The youth leader should make sure that his teens attend one week each summer at an organized camp, even though he may need to take them a thousand miles in a chartered bus (since the typical church bus is too rough and undependable for extended trips). In addition, the youth leader ought to plan several weekend retreats each year in the fall or spring or even during the vacation time between Christmas and New Year's Day. Most organized camps hold these retreats, but a youth leader could run his own, getting the parents to help put it on. The ingredients necessary for organizing a camp or retreat are as follows.

Facilities

Some organized camps or private camps will lease their facilities in the off-season, or it is possible for church groups to rent the facilities at a state park. Adequate sleeping, kitchen, dining, and recreational facilities should be available. Also, there should be a large meeting room, preferably with a fireplace, for the messages, although the dining hall can be used for meetings if it has movable chairs and tables.

Speakers

An outside voice has a greater impact at these retreats than the youth leader would have, even if that voice is just another youth leader or the pastor of a church within a hundred miles. It is best to have two messages on Friday night, one of which might be a film; two on Saturday morning; two on Saturday evening, one of which is a campfire service; and one on Sunday morning with a testimony time. Gospel and dedication emphases throughout the retreat or camp build toward the climax of the Saturday night campfire service. This service is the main invitation and decision time.

On a retreat or a camp, adults should go along to act as counselors and authority figures in the cabins. The youth leader must then pray that the Holy Spirit does His work in the campers' hearts.

Food

The ladies of the church can provide some of the food, or several women can go along to cook. The key is to keep the meals simple and easy to prepare. A sample weekend menu is as follows:

Friday evening meal: hot dogs, potato chips, carrots, celery strips, cake, milk, and pop.
Friday midnight snack: hot chocolate and cookies

Saturday breakfast: oranges, ham and eggs, toast, and milk
Saturday noon: soup, sandwiches, corn chips, pie, milk, and pop

Saturday evening: hamburgers or pizza, potato chips, tomatoes, apples, ice cream bars, milk, and pop

Saturday midnight snack: popcorn and pop

Sunday breakfast: individual boxes of cereal, orange juice or oranges, sweet rolls, and milk

Sunday noon: meat loaf or fried chicken, scalloped potatoes (prepared ahead by the ladies of the church and reheated at the camp), green beans, salad, cake, milk, and pop

Those in charge should buy everything wholesale when possible, looking for specials on crates of apples, oranges, pop, and potato chips. The local wholesale food distributor can give good advice and help. Using paper plates, cups, and plastic utensils eliminates the problems of dishwashing.

Programs and recreation

On Friday night after supper, there should be an hour of competition, dividing the teens into several teams and having each team devise its own name and cheer. Sure-fire competitions include indoor scavenger hunts (for hairs, toenails, etc.), relays (passing a Lifesaver on a straw), or pig-outs (eating without using hands or utensils a chocolate meringue pie placed on the floor). Other popular games are three-man skiing, mattress relays, marathon relays, or big-ball competition. Keep the team enthusiasm high by keeping score and giving prizes to the winning team. A midnight hike to the top of a mountain, if the moon is full and the path is clear, might be appropriate.

Recreation should be planned for Saturday afternoon, including ball games, swimming, skiing, hiking, Ping-Pong, or whatever the area provides. If a volleyball net is set up near the main meeting area, the kids will keep volleyball games going the whole weekend. Good group activities will stress team involvement and effort. The Wilds's S.O.A.P. books will give the leader hundreds of ideas for exciting activities.

On Saturday night each team should put on a humorous skit. In addition, each team could be provided with one roll of toilet paper and some newspapers to decorate one of its members. Enthusiastic singing times and a dynamic speaker round out a weekend program.

Equipment

The youth leader must make a list of all the equipment that will have to be taken along. The extent of the list depends on what the camp facilities provide, but it will probably include cooking pans, soap and toilet paper, first-aid kits, recreation equipment, a film projector, and the items needed for the Friday night competition.

Transportation and publicity

Adequate buses or cars must be procured and the appropriate pickup points assigned. The youth leader should distribute a fact sheet that lists the time, the place, directions, what to bring, and other pertinent information. The leader should obtain a nonrefundable down payment from each teen to ensure the teen's attendance. He should promote the retreat two months ahead, posting pictures of past retreats to create enthusiasm.

Other Kinds of Camps

Planning a wilderness camp, a missionary trip (camping out along the way), or a super trip (such as hiking down to the bottom of Grand Canyon and camping out) takes much more planning and preparation, but the six steps above would still apply.

Many churches are getting their people into family camps, couples' retreats, and separate men's and women's retreats, where a specific emphasis can be given to contribute to family unity. A family that spends its vacation at a camp or in other spiritually uplifting surroundings can have an inexpensive but rewarding time of family strengthening. For example, each summer Bob Jones University hosts a program for families called Peace-Full Vacation. Families stay for a week in the dorms and eat in the dining hall. They enjoy all the recreational activities and facilities, take side trips, and attend special Bible classes, workshops, and training sessions on subjects such as gourmet cooking, novelty woodworking, and home computers. This program is not a camp in the strict sense of the word, but it accomplishes many of the same purposes that camps have.

Encourage families to use their vacation times to go to a mission field for a week or two of real service. Families should take camping equipment and food so that they are not a burden to the missionaries.

For a church or even several churches to own their own camp is not always feasible; the overhead, maintenance, and staffing can be a financial drain. For the amount of camping that the average church does, it is best to patronize organized camps or to rent facilities.

Camping can be a wonderful asset to the youth director's goals for his teen-agers. A bit of creative imagination and planning and wise use of available facilities will enhance a local church youth ministry and bring eternal benefits.

Chapter 9
The Ministry of Music: A Necessary "Extra"

Music is second only to preaching and teaching as a means of communicating the gospel message to teen-agers and motivating them to full-time service. If Satan can upset and corrupt the music program, he has an opportunity to corrupt the whole gospel program. But properly used, music is the most effective vehicle for preparing teens' hearts to receive the Word. Not only are some of the most treasured memories of revival and decision times brought to mind by a familiar song, but also the words of a song can bring comfort in times of stress and hardship. For these reasons songs used in the youth ministry should be related to Scripture or contain Scripture.

Teen-agers respond to music that stirs and affects their emotions, hence the popularity of love songs and rock music. One study found that teens listen to the radio an average of fourteen hours a week and to rock music a total of twenty-eight hours a week. Youth leaders can capitalize on this appetite for the sake of the gospel, but they must set standards to avoid the pitfall of catering to the teens' fleshly nature and worldly desires. Philippians 1:9-10 gives a standard of excellence to use as a guide: "And this I pray, that your love may abound yet more and more in knowledge and in all judgment; That ye may approve things that are excellent; that ye may be sincere and without offense till the day of

Christ." Rather than trying to draw a line between the acceptable and the unacceptable, the youth leader should help the teens discern and seek after the most excellent things, the things that will uplift and bring them closer to God. Ephesians 5:10 emphasizes the necessity of "proving what is acceptable unto the Lord."

Principles

Certain principles are crucial in setting music standards, and they can be discerned even by one who has not been trained in music.

Text

The words should clearly present Bible truth and even contain Scripture if possible. The great songs and hymns of the past that have stood the test of time upheld Jesus Christ as Lord and emphasized Bible truth. Songs of personal testimony can be effective if the message of the song emphasizes Bible truth instead of just a person's feelings (e.g., "No One Ever Cared for Me Like Jesus"). The songs should avoid slang expressions and words which are in the teen vernacular. Referring to God as "The All-Right Man," "Big Daddy," "The Man Upstairs," and "My Buddy Jesus" does not honor God or give the teens the right view of the Almighty God whom they worship. Jesus Christ is the "friend that sticketh closer than a brother" (Prov. 18:24), but still He is God, and He is to be glorified and praised. The standard of Colossians 3:16 can be used to judge the words of our gospel music: "Let the word of Christ dwell in you richly in all wisdom; teaching and admonishing one another in psalms and hymns and spiritual songs, singing with grace in your hearts to the Lord."

Tune

The music shapes the words as the pie pan and crust determine the shape of the pie filling. Music that is appropriate to the text and balanced in melody, harmony, rhythm, and dynamics (volume) provides a vehicle that carries the message of God to the soul. It uplifts and directs the spirit in line with Ephesians 5:19: "Speaking to yourselves in psalms and hymns and spiritual songs, singing and making melody in your heart to the Lord." Melody speaks to man's spirit; harmony, to the soul or mind; and rhythm, to the body. The right music can set the attitude of the spirit and mind to allow the Holy Spirit to bring about conviction of sin and judgment (John 16:7-11).

The contemporary sound—which may involve blues, jazz, swing, country-western ballad, folk, soul, or any combination thereof—tends to create a vehicle that has distracting worldly associations. It detracts from the message of God and brings unproductive and unwholesome thoughts and feelings. The "hurtin'" songs in country music are such vehicles. Even though this music is often sentimental because of its cultural-ethnic origins, its style is incongruous with the Christian message. It brings back memories of worldly entertainment and places—television programs, movies, bars, dances, and the Broadway stage. Romans 12:2 plainly advises us not to have worldly associations as a part of our life pattern.

Some musically superior ballad-style tunes can be used to good effect. For example, some churches use the tune of "The Happy Wanderer" with the words of "O for a Thousand Tongues to Sing." Tunes should be positive and uplifting and free from association with corrupt words or situations. For example, putting Christian words to the tunes of Scott Joplin or the swing band sound of the forties might be sentimental to some people, but the combination is rather incongruous. Choosing depressing or unsavory tunes is like delivering the gospel message in a manure truck.

Rock music is not a viable musical vehicle for uplifting, God-honoring words. Its deliberate, insistent, unrestrained repetition of syncopated off-beat rhythms and basic chord patterns prompts a physical response and stirs up a spirit of lawlessness in the hearer. It was no accident that rock music was predominant in the lawless sixties.

The term *rock and roll* was coined by Alan Freed, a disc jockey on WJW in Cleveland, Ohio, and the phrase is street talk for an act of illicit, lustful sex. It was popularized in 1956 by Bill Haley and his Comets in the song "Rock Around the Clock." The strong, insistent beat, repeated chords, and loud volume trigger the release of adrenaline and sex hormones in the body, stirring up the sex impulses and emotions, putting teens in the mood for all kinds of immorality and corruption. They get addicted to the so-called natural high, and many go further to seek artificial highs in drugs. Rock musicians boast that their music, with its sex and drug-related words, brought free sex and drugs down to the junior and senior high teens between 1965 and 1970. Most youth evangelists have found that teens who are addicted to rock music and vigorously defend it have problems with immorality in their lives. Because of the immorality of the music itself and its corrupt associations, saying that there is Christian rock is like saying there is such a thing as Christian pornography or Christian gambling.

The rock beat, combined with its repetitious loud sounds, stimulates the mind to build up body energy, producing an intense emotional state. This energy demands release, and the release comes through body action in wild gyrations, sexual manifestations, and other abnormal behavior. Some have suggested that it can lead to demonic control; watching the actions of the performers and audience would seem to verify these conclusions. II Corinthians 10:5 gives clear direction for the type of thinking that we should discard, and Philippians 4:8 states what kind of thoughts we should stimulate. Rock music is a tremendous stimulator of evil thoughts, and good music is a superior stimulant for the right thoughts.[1]

Performance

The way music is performed affects the message. The old "pray-for-me-while-I-sing-because-I-haven't-practiced" routine would be laughable if it were not so common. Adequate preparation and practice is an essential requirement for every performance. Affectation and egotistical overemphasis on techniques also distract from the message. The vulgar, nightclub showmanship—the intimate, sensual, "licking the microphone" style, magnifying every breath and sigh, eliciting clapping and whistling—does not have a place in a worthy gospel outreach. Music should be performed much as a preacher preaches the Word, with reverence and humility and in the power of the Spirit, so that the audience will be blessed, challenged, and motivated to do right. First Corinthians 10:31 should be the guide if the performance is going to measure up to God's standard.

Sources

The right songbooks and musical arrangements are prerequisites for a high-quality music program. Most music writers, arrangers, and publishers cater to the public's tastes in order to make a profit. As a consequence, much of today's gospel music reflects the worldly, corrupt, sensual attitudes that result from excessive television viewing by the average Christian. Also, since most of the parents of the teens were "rock-and-roll" teens in their youth, they may negatively affect the standards of their children. Youth leaders have a responsibility to change and upgrade the teens' music standards.

The job can be done by getting high-quality song and chorus books with proper arrangements for youth choirs and music groups. Recommendable song books are *We're Singing in The Wilds,*[2] *Praises,*[3] and *The Bill Rice Ranch Songbook.*[4] Majesty Music, Inc. also publishes a book of teen choir arrangements entitled *Joysong.* Songbooks and songs compiled and written by Al Smith are, like the above, heart-warming, in good taste, and appropriate for the average person's level of musical knowledge and potential. Sword of the Lord Publications publishes a collection entitled *Soul Stirring Songs and Hymns* that is used by many youth groups and choirs.

Purpose

While on furlough a few years ago, the director of a large, well-known youth work in Brazil wrote to Al Smith. The following excerpts from his letter show what can be accomplished with youth when an honest attempt is made to bring a music program into line with God's standards, approving "things that are excellent."

Dear Al:

As you know, I have been in Brazil for some twenty-three years and most of that time . . . involved with youth ministry. It has been our desire to reach the Brazilian youth with the message of Jesus Christ to see if we can win that great mission field for the Lord. We have seen wonderful things happen and we believe that there is a real hope for that country. One of the ways by which we minister to the young people is through the medium of music. We have young people down there who love to play their guitars, sing, form ensembles, choirs, and quartets and trios just like here in this country. We have used these groups many times in our rallies and in visiting high schools and places where young people congregate, and we try through word and music to win them to the Lord. We followed for some time a pattern which had become a sort of standard with all such groups that was basically singing folk songs and popular type music to get their ear. We felt that if we could get them to listen to us, . . . we would have a chance to tell them about the Lord. We also felt that if we started out by singing hymns, they would immediately turn us off, since that is not what the average teen-ager who does not love the Lord is looking for.

But little by little I had misgivings about this whole philosophy. I felt . . . that it was sort of a sneaky way to reach them and that many of these teen-agers certainly are not dumb. I looked at this as being somewhat dishonest. They would know before the meeting was over that our real reason for being there was not to entertain them with good music, but to "push a religion," as they would say. And presented that way, it did not make our religion seem very honorable. So instead of accomplishing our goal, we were actually defeating it.

There was another thing that troubled me. I felt that, indirectly, we were teaching something that was definitely not Scriptural: that there is a point of compatibility between the world and the Christian life. Galatians 6:14, James 4:4, I John 2:15 and 16, Romans 12:2, and many other verses clearly state that the world and Christ are poles apart and that the only point of contact between the two is in the attitude of total surrender on the part of the world at the foot of the cross. I felt that if we went about trying to communicate Christ's message using the world's methods and the world's type of music, . . . we were, indirectly, saying to the young people that you can bring about a sort of happy, peaceful co-existence between Christ and the world. That idea, although not taught by us as evangelicals as such, is frequently being communicated indirectly; and that idea, I believe, is diametrically opposed to the basic teachings of our blessed Lord and Savior, Jesus Christ.

So (last year) we had a new group coming to work with us composed of four fellows and four girls. I told them that we were going to embark on an experiment. I told them that we would sing only hymns—not necessarily just the old hymns but newer hymns too; however, we would sing only songs that would be readily identified as sacred songs and make no attempt whatsoever to try to copy the popular singing groups and the world's heroes. The young people, understandably, were rather frightened with the prospects. They thought that they would be literally hooted from the platform on their first song. However, I did challenge them with this prospect, telling them that if for the sake of Christ we were to be rejected, then at least we would be rejected in an honorable way. I also told them that if in our stand for the Lord Jesus Christ the world rejects us or persecutes us, it is not a reason for shame, but for joy—I Peter 4:14 and 16. On the other hand, I told them that I didn't think the young people in the high schools would reject them. I really felt that if we were very open about it and told them that we were there to tell them about the Lord and made no effort to camouflage our real motives, . . . we would be even more readily acceptable to them.

Forming a New Generation

After a day of Bible study and prayer together, . . . they finally agreed to go with me on this experiment for one year. The results were overwhelming. Not even I had believed that it would work so well. We sang in hundreds of high schools in which the vast majority (up to 90 or 95 per cent) were unconverted teen-agers. They are normally just as rowdy and unruly as Americans. But in every high school that we visited, with only one exception (and this was in a so-called Christian high school), we had an attentive audience during the whole forty-five minutes of our presentation. I would start the program with a short word of introduction, saying that our purpose in being in that particular high school was to tell them about . . . Jesus Christ and how He had affected our lives and what He could do in their lives. I said that the means of our communicating the message of Jesus Christ would be through song (and that I believed they would enjoy the songs) and through personal testimonies on the part of our singers and a short message from God's word. . . . In other words, we put all the cards on the table.

We did rehearse a lot and put on the very finest music that we could, but we never tried to disguise it in the world's forms. We tried to keep our testimonies short, very straightforward and to the point, without bending over backwards in order to be entertaining. There is no doubt in my mind today that this is the right way to do it. When the year was over, I asked the fellows and girls in our group what they thought of the experience, and all of them . . . wholeheartedly agreed that they would never go back to doing it any other way. God has given us a noble and exciting message to proclaim, and I believe we should be straightforward in presenting it.

What I have challenged the young people on our staff to do is to eliminate, as much as they possibly can, all forms of music that would not be inspiring from the spiritual standpoint. I asked them to not only eliminate worldly music, popular songs, etc., but also to listen to hymns as often as they could—just starting the day and ending the day and during the day whenever they have an opportunity to listen to . . . hymns. We also have included classical songs as a possible variance in this diet. I had asked my staff to do this for one week to see if they noticed any difference in their spiritual lives. Without exception, they have all commented that they have noticed a definite improvement in their spiritual lives and in their personal relationship to the Lord.

A number of our staff have already destroyed their other records and are building . . . a library of sacred songs. They are convinced that the only way to total Christian commitment, to a total nonconformity with a wicked world system, is through a total renewal of mind. We are physically in this world, but we do not become a part of it in any way. Al, I know that sounds like a very idealistic and perhaps unrealistic thing to say, and I would not venture to say that I've made the grade, but it is a goal toward which we are striving.

Just one more thing I'd like to share with you, Al, and that is, in our desire to present music that would be honoring to the Lord and edifying to the church and at the same time not be tied exclusively to that which has been written in the past, we have challenged our Brazilian young people to write songs. Most of what we do in Brazil is now original music produced by Brazilian young people. I've challenged them to get their inspiration from God's Word. In other words, to steep themselves in Scripture until they burst out in song.

Al, it seems to me that somehow Satan has succeeded in getting us suckered out in an area that is innocent in first appearance, but devastating in its influence. The battle that Satan could not win in the pulpits of the evangelical churches, he is winning through the choir. The powerful dynamic of obedience, self-denial, and cross bearing is giving way to showmanship and entertainment. I really believe that if Satan can get us to sing his songs, even if we do put so-called Christian words to them, he's got the battle made.

This letter shows what can be accomplished with godly leadership in the music program. Why can't the same musical standards be set for youth groups here in America?

Other Considerations

Selections

A song service should always be prepared with the message and the audience in mind. A youth evangelistic service with many unsaved in attendance would require totally different music from a campfire dedication service for Christians. A song service should have different types of songs and a pace varied by different tempos, keys, and types of songs. Listed in Appendix I are seven classifications of songs with a few suggested titles. The challenge and action songs should come at the start of the service, working up to the more serious songs before the message. Most of the songs listed are found in Al Smith's *Living Hymns,* the *Praises* book, or the Wilds songbook.

Accompaniment

A good pianist is essential to good musical programs and good group singing. A pianist who can emphasize the tempo and rhythm will make a song service come alive. Pitching the song lower will accommodate both men's and women's voices on some difficult numbers. A guitar or ukelele would be appropriate for an outdoor meeting or campfire service.

Setting

Singing around a campfire is a tremendous heart-touching and memory-building experience, especially if it is related to God's mighty works in nature. Hearing the croak of the frog or the chirp of the cricket and seeing the Big Dipper and the North Star hanging over the lake while the group sings "How Great Thou Art" helps teens develop right attitudes toward God.

Goals

An effort should be made to develop the musical potential and natural interest for music in your group. A leader with basic musical abilities can teach the teens songleading techniques and let them lead teen services. Duets, trios, and quartets should be formed and many opportunities provided for them to perform. A youth choir, youth ensembles, youth instrumental ensembles, or an orchestra can have a continuing weekly ministry. In addition, teen solo instrumental numbers can be effective as offertories, especially if the audience follows the words in the hymnbook.

An effective youth leader should use music as a vital part of the evangelistic and edification program. It will not only prove to be a good tool, but it will also enrich and broaden the teens' Christian cultural perspective. Everything possible should be done to help teens develop good record and tape collections of sacred and classical music. After a life-changing teen revival, where good music standards are preached, provide a record and tape burning for corrupt music. The church bookstore should have good tapes and records available so that parents can buy them for the teens' Christmas and birthday presents. The youth leader must give assistance in helping teens to decide between the holy and the profane and between the clean and the unclean (Ezekiel 22:26; 44:23) just as the priests were to do in the Old Testament. He must help them to have knowledge and good judgment about music so that they "may approve things that are excellent."

The leader can make a contribution to gospel musical heritage and good Biblical musical standards by giving discerning attention to this vital area of his ministry. He must remember that the teens in the typical church of today will be the parents ten to twenty years hence, and the standards they adopt now will affect future generations.

Forming a New Generation

---

[1] The *Symphony of Life* seminar tapes by Frank Garlock are available from Majesty Music, Inc., PO Box 5624, Greenville, SC 29606, and should be used for training sessions on music.

[2] Write The Wilds, 3180 Wade Hampton Blvd., Taylors, SC 29687.

[3] Write Majesty Music, Inc. (See address above.)

[4] Write The Bill Rice Ranch, Murfreesboro, TN 37130.

Chapter 10
The Soulwinning Challenge: Motivating Youth to Evangelize

One of the main purposes of the church is to evangelize. Evangelism is not just winning souls but is also discipling those new converts—discipling them to study the Word of God, to grow in faith, to become soulwinners, and to contribute their time, talents, and money to the local church in spreading the gospel worldwide. If a youth group is going to grow and if the teens are going to glorify God, they must be involved in a comprehensive program of evangelism. The "professionals" —the youth leader and the pastor—cannot reach all the people in a given locality. Lay people are needed to win souls for Jesus Christ; therefore, evangelism must be a main emphasis with the youth.

Evangelism is the task of every Christian. Acts 8:1 says that "they were all scattered abroad except the apostles" during the great persecution of the church. Then Acts 8:4 explains, "Therefore they that were scattered abroad went everywhere preaching the Word." It was laymen that were preaching the Word. One large youth organization in its survey of thousands of Christian teen-agers found that thirty-four per cent of those teens had been won to Christ by a close friend. Teens reaching teens is the best way to win teens.

Prerequisites

Before training soulwinners, the leader himself must be a soulwinner. He must be convinced of the necessity of evangelism. If he has never led a person to Jesus Christ, he is going to have difficulty training soulwinners in the youth group. His example, his leading the way, will turn his youth into soulwinners. As the youth group begins to increase, the leader will be highly motivated to prepare effective training lessons and challenging activities to service this growing crowd. Those in the youth group who are trying to win souls will become motivated to start praying, have regular devotions, and study their Bibles for answers to the questions that they face in their soulwinning contacts and in discipling new converts.

In addition, the leader must put into practice the multiplication principle found in II Timothy 2:2: "And the things that thou hast heard of me among many witnesses, the same commit thou to faithful men, who shall be able to teach others also." If a Christian were to win a soul every six months, at the end of five years he would have won ten people to Jesus Christ. However, if each of those converts had been trained to win souls for the Lord, the result would be far different. If each one, without exception, were winning and training one person every six months, there would be 1,024 converts at the end of five years. That would be quite a youth group, even if just one tenth of those joined the group. Instead of seeing souls increase mathematically, the youth leader would see them increase geometrically.[1]

Motivating

Teens must be continually challenged to win souls. Matthew 28:19-20; Mark 16:15; John 15:16; and Acts 1:8 all contain challenges from the Lord to witness.

Psalm 126:6 contains as good a parallel to the task of soulwinning as any passage: "He that goeth forth and weepeth, bearing precious seed, shall doubtless come again with rejoicing, bringing his sheaves with him." First, *he* indicates that it takes individual, born-again Christians to do the work of soulwinning. Second, *that goeth forth* is a charge to reach out—to go where people are. Third, *weepeth* refers to verse 5: "They that sow in tears shall reap in joy." A soulwinner will have a heart concern and a willingness to make sacrifices to try to reach people. That concern will make him go out into the cold on snowy days, and it will make him go out on wet days and hot days as the Holy Spirit leads him to certain places to talk to certain people. Teen-agers (and their youth leaders) need to say every day, "Oh, Lord, lead me to some soul today. I'm ready to win souls." Fourth, *bearing precious seed* reminds the soulwinner that he has to go forth with the Word of God. "Faith cometh by hearing, and hearing by the word of God" (Romans 10:17); so as the Word of God is used, God's power begins to work in a life. It is not words, not stories, but the Word of God that cuts to the heart (Hebrews 4:12). The final step is found in the last part of Psalm 126:6: "shall doubtless come . . . , bringing his sheaves with him." This portion indicates that the soulwinner will see fruit for his labor. Souls will be saved if he faithfully gives out the Word of God.

Romans 1:14-16 contains another challenge to evangelism. It delineates three steps to becoming a soulwinner. Paul says, "I am debtor both to the Greeks and to the barbarians, both to the wise and to the unwise." When Paul received the gospel, he realized that he had a debt to others who had not received Jesus Christ as their Saviour.

In verse 15 Paul says, "As much as in me is, I am ready to preach the gospel." Like Paul, born-again Christians must be ready to give out tracts, ready to write letters to friends and relatives, ready to witness in the office, on the job, over the telephone, on business trips, on pleasure trips, wherever they meet people. People they meet are either saved or lost. If they are saved, the soulwinner can edify them and have fellowship with them. If they are lost, they can be given the gospel. Paul was always ready.

And then in verse 16 Paul says, "For I am not ashamed of the gospel of Christ, for it is the power of God unto salvation to every one that believeth, to the Jew first and also to the Greek." The main reason people do not declare the simple way of salvation is that they are ashamed of the gospel, ashamed mainly because of the persecution that they fear. Every Christian must realize that he is going to be persecuted if he declares the gospel of Jesus Christ.

Teen-agers need to be warned that the minute they start living a life for Christ, separating themselves from the corruption of the world, and witnessing, they are going to have persecution. I Peter 4:2-4 says that when a Christian departs from the fleshly lusts of men to do the will of God, people are going to think it strange that he does not enjoy the same things they enjoy, and they are going to start speaking evil of him. At that point the Christian must ask himself if he has a sweet testimony of love or if he reflects the evil spirit of the persecutor. I Peter 4:12-16 tells a Christian not to be surprised at this persecution as if it were not supposed to happen. When a teen-ager begins to give out the gospel, he is going to be reproached for the name of Christ. He is going to suffer as a Christian—maybe not physically but at least psychologically—and he should not be ashamed. John 15:16-20 indicates that when a Christian starts bearing fruit, the world is going to hate him. It hated Jesus Christ first, and "the servant is not greater than his lord" (John 15:20). If the people persecuted Christ, they will also persecute the Christian, especially when he keeps Christ's sayings and follows His will by holding forth the Word of Life.

Christians will not be ashamed if they realize the tremendous power of the gospel. As the Scripture emphasizes, "It is the power of God unto salvation to everyone that believeth, to the Jew first and also to the Greek "(Romans 1:16). This powerful gospel overcomes the two greatest fears of mankind. Hebrews 9:27 says, "It is appointed unto men once to die, but after this the judgment." All people have a basic fear of death and judgment, but the gospel and salvation take away that fear. Born-again Christians are no longer under the terrible wrath of God (Romans 8:1). Instead of worrying about the little opposition and persecution that they may receive, they can boldly preach the gospel of Jesus Christ. People will become angry, but believers must keep on preaching the gospel to them, knowing that many will receive Jesus Christ as their personal Saviour.

Another challenge for evangelism is found in II Corinthians 5:11-20. Verse 11 says, "Knowing therefore the terror of the Lord, we persuade men," and then verse 14 adds, "For the love of Christ constraineth us." These are two great motivations for the soulwinner. First, knowing the terror of the Lord against sinners, the soulwinner must present the gospel. Second, knowing Christ's love for sinners, he must witness about that love. If Christ were willing to die for all men, the Christian certainly ought to be willing to tell others about His sacrifice. Verse 14 continues, "If one died for all, then were all dead." Every Christian has the life-saving remedy that will cure people of this dread sin disease.

Verse 15 indicates that the Christian should not live for himself but rather for Christ. Verse 17 declares that the Christian is a new creature in Christ Jesus; the old selfish desires have passed away, and all things have become new. There are new attitudes and new visions. He needs to see people as they really are—not as heroes to be emulated in lifestyle, dress, and worldly attitudes, but rather as condemned human beings who are going to an eternal hell and who need rescuing. Verse 18 indicates that God has given to the Christian the ministry of reconciling people to Christ. Verse 20 shows plainly that he is an ambassador for Christ and a representative of the Heavenly King in this foreign land, holding forth the message of Jesus Christ and His shed blood that can make a sinner completely righteous before God.

The youth leader should challenge teens to give out the "gospel sandwich" to satisfy the hunger of lost sinners. The bottom piece of bread in the gospel sandwich is the friendly spirit, getting acquainted and being interested in the lost person. The meat of the sandwich is six to eight verses explaining salvation (Romans 3:23; 6:23; 5:8; Ephesians 2:8-9;

John 1:12; Revelation 3:20; I John 5:11-13; and/or Romans 10:13). The top piece of bread is giving the sinner the opportunity to accept Christ as his Saviour.

Teen-agers need this challenge of soulwinning before they need the techniques, and the challenge must be based on personal salvation. Since many so-called Christians and church members in fundamentalist churches are not saved, they have no interest whatever in getting the gospel out to every creature. No one can give out something that he hasn't received. When there is no motivation for soulwinning—no enthusiasm, no zeal—a leader should suspect that the person is either unsaved or has terrible sin in his life (Psalm 51:12-15), even though he may be a deacon, a church officer, a Sunday school teacher, or a faithful worker in the church. If he is not interested in declaring the gospel of Jesus Christ, he probably has never received it himself.

Teaching

If evangelism must be one of the main goals in the youth group, then training teens in evangelism should be one of the main tasks. Teen-age soulwinning training can be classified into five phases of evangelism with increasing difficulty for the individual teen-ager.

Phase one would be the simple act of inviting people out to church, the youth meeting, or some gospel service. Several large churches have taken surveys of the souls that were saved in their church services and found that most of the new converts were visitors (eighty-seven per cent in one study) who had been invited by church members. The same percentage will hold true in the youth group. Unsaved teens will generally not come to the youth meetings unless they are invited by one of the other teens. As teens invite other teens for services, the youth evangelistic service in particular, they get to see these teens saved as a result of the Holy Spirit's working through the leader's message, the testimonies of the group, and their own personal witness to the visitor. As the teens see the power of the gospel change people's lives, they become highly motivated. As an increasing number of teen-agers come out to hear the youth leader's message and the pastor's sermons, many will become converted. This response in turn will build the youth group and motivate the whole church in evangelism.

Phase two in soulwinning training is motivating the teen-agers to start giving out tracts. This is a more difficult and bolder witness. In one approach, teens make an agreement with the Lord to pass out at least one or two tracts every single week, personally giving the tract to a friend or somebody they may meet. Studies have shown that about one of every hundred tract recipients is converted. Sometimes, teens attending a public school may band together and decide to put a tract in every locker or to hand out tracts to everyone they know at school. The next step may be handing out tracts in shopping centers and putting a tract and some information about their local church on the doorknob of every house in the town or in the county. Some teens hand out a tract every time they get gas or go into a store. A whole town can be blitzed by gospel tracts in a short time when teens commit themselves to the job.

Phase three of soulwinning is giving a gospel testimony directly to others. Whenever a teen is alone with a person for any length of time, he presents the claims of Christ. This phase is a little more difficult for teen-agers; it requires some holy boldness. In this phase the teen talks to a person and gives testimony of his salvation, reading aloud or quoting the verses that people used to lead him to Christ, telling how he reacted, what he thought, and what he did about it. These personal testimonies of salvation can be a powerful influence on unsaved people. The teens can start by giving their testimonies in the youth group or before the church. Later they might give testimonies at various street meetings, jail services, and rescue mission services. They can also put their gospel testimonies in letters to relatives and friends.

Phase four is getting a target individual, winning a person to the Lord Jesus Christ, and then discipling him. The phase starts by inviting and taking an unsaved person to Sunday school, church services, youth meetings, and activities. It continues as the teen gives a personal witness whenever possible and even goes to the point of fasting and praying for the target individual (who may be a friend or some loved one). Once that person has been led to Jesus Christ, the teen-ager sets out to disciple him. The teen in this way becomes a II Timothy 2:2 discipler, something few people in the church ever achieve.

The discipler has a regular Bible study with the convert, becomes a real friend, takes him to church and out soul-winning, encourages him to memorize verses, and does everything he can to build him up in the faith. It takes determination, commitment, and singlemindedness. Soul-winning makes a great difference in the life of a teen-ager, changing him into a real gospel worker. Now he is ready for phase five.

Phase five is becoming involved in some gospel ministry, such as testifying or preaching in a jail service, a rescue mission service, or a street meeting. Teens can teach Sunday school classes, work on the bus route, or hold child evangelism clubs in their neighborhood. The youth leader may schedule various groups of teens for street meetings on Saturdays, a jail service, or a service in the children's home, orphanage, or nursing home. Many times rescue missions are willing to let the local fundamentalist church have a service one night a month. The teens can put on this service, doing the singing, preaching, and giving their testimonies. They can also go in the summer on gospel teams to churches or to mission fields, especially if there are two or three talented musicians and one or two young men that can preach. They can also have public high school Bible clubs meeting in the evenings in their home as a part of youth ministry outreach. The youth director coordinates these clubs, which feed into the youth group. The teens can even put on a weekly gospel radio program.

Implementing

The youth leader is the one responsible for providing the opportunities, the materials, and the motivation for teen-agers to put the phases into action in their own lives. For a continuing implementation of phase one, for example, the youth group could hold special activities at least once a month where teens can invite others. The leader would give special recognition or even prizes for the teen who invites the most people. Invited visitors should be recognized, and the teen-ager should stand with each person he invited. Once a year, on a weekend or one week in the summer, many churches have the Minutemen Evangelistic Team from Bob Jones University come to put on "The War." This activity involves the teens in an all-out community-wide evangelistic effort, and hundreds of teens can be reached.[2]

For phase two, a supply of appropriate tracts must be available for the teens, and the young people should report every week the number of tracts they gave out. To challenge teens with tract-passing, the leader can present to the group testimonies of people being saved after reading tracts or ask some teens to give testimonies of how they distributed tracts and the results of these endeavors.

In developing the third phase, the youth director would take new converts out soulwinning, having them give their testimonies of how they were saved. These new converts should immediately learn five or six salvation verses that they can use in their testimony. The older Christian teens who have been saved for a while should learn five or six soulwinning verses and write out a soulwinning testimony that they can give as they go out soulwinning. The survey technique can be used to reach all the teens in town. (See Appendix H-1.)

In phase four the youth leader should train the teens on how to target a teen or friend, win him to the Lord, and then disciple the new convert. They are given materials and instruction for a proper follow-up and discipleship program.

The youth leader can promote phase five by forming teen gospel teams and by scheduling services and missionary trips where the teens can sing, perform, preach, and spread the gospel. These activities would include even summer missionary tours. As the teens get into phase five, they should be challenged to make soulwinning, mission work, and preaching their full-time occupation.

Techniques

The survey technique is an excellent technique for getting started in evangelism and soulwinning. It is especially good for teens who go to Christian schools and do not come into contact with unsaved teens. This technique is a means for the teen to get into a home and get a spiritual conversation started. It helps to break down the social barrier that stops most new converts from becoming soulwinners. The teens go out two by two, knocking on doors and asking whether there are any teens in the home. They then ask those teens if they would like to be part of a religious survey. The survey is a printed series of questions on a form, starting out with the person's name and address and then several personal questions, such as the ones asked in Appendix H-1. All the teen-agers taking the survey are trained to present six or eight verses from the Word of God and to know what to do to lead a soul to Jesus Christ.

Whatever the system of verses a soulwinner uses—the Romans Road verses, the Navigator verses, the Evangelism Explosion verses, or others—he declares certain ideas. Man is a sinner and needs a Saviour. He cannot save himself, and there is a terrible judgment coming upon sin. Jesus Christ died on the cross for man's sin, shedding His precious blood as a payment for that sin. He is the resurrected Saviour who has the power to save men from sin because of His resurrection. Sinners must not only believe these truths but also repent (or turn from their sins) and receive Jesus Christ as personal Saviour. Many soulwinners use John 1:12 and

I John 5:11-13 to present this idea of receiving Christ as the important final decision for salvation.

Many people in mainline denominations and even in Catholicism believe in the virgin birth and the deity of Jesus Christ. They believe in the death, burial, and resurrection of Jesus Christ; they celebrate Christmas and Easter; and they do not do it in a superficial way. It has real meaning for them. As far as they know, they do believe in Jesus Christ. But there has never been a time in their lives when they have received Jesus Christ as their Saviour, trusting in Him and Him alone for their salvation. They have never had the experience of being born again but are instead trusting in their church membership or their works to get them to heaven.

After clearly presenting the gospel, the soulwinner gives the person an opportunity to receive Jesus Christ as his personal Saviour. This closing is usually in the form of a question: "Would you like to receive Jesus Christ as your personal Saviour now?" Most people will give all kinds of excuses: they want to wait awhile; they want to think the thing through; they don't want to do it right now. But they need to be urged to receive Jesus Christ as their personal Saviour by faith right at that time. It is best not to use psychological techniques on them or get them emotionally wrought up. Just give them the simple opportunity to receive Christ. They can either accept or reject it at that time. Approaching them with that decision, however, is a very crucial thing. They need to realize that if they do not accept Jesus Christ, they remain in their sin and face the certain prospect of hell if they should die as they are. People must be shown plainly what to do with the gospel, even if they do not then make the decision to accept Christ.

The Holy Spirit will work in the heart in the intervening time if they do not make a decision. Many people do get under conviction when they hear the gospel, and they want to think about it over a period of days or weeks. The Holy Spirit's convicting power gets stronger and stronger until finally they do receive Christ. The soulwinner tries to make himself available to that person who has received the gospel witness so he can help him when he is finally ready to receive Christ.

In order for the survey to be valid, the leader must keep the statistics from the teens' answers on the survey forms. For example, the surveys that the authors have recorded over many years show that only about a third of the teen-agers questioned have the slightest idea of how to get to heaven. Most will give works as the way to heaven.

The completed survey forms will become part of a prospect file. The forms should be grouped by areas of the town so that a thorough follow-up can be made on these people. The file will give many prospects for return visits and also many prospects for the youth group.

Discipleship

Follow-up and discipleship are as important as soul-winning. Taking the II Timothy 2:2 point of view with any new convert makes that new convert a reproducer. The first step is to get back with the new convert within twenty-four hours and once a week thereafter to answer questions and help him get started in Bible reading and study. Next, the convert should be encouraged to make a public profession, be baptized, and attend a good Bible-preaching church. The next step is to get him memorizing Scripture. The first verses should be those that will help him in his Christian growth; the next should be verses that will help him win souls to Christ. The final step is to take the new convert out soulwinning and then to get him out on his own winning souls and discipling them. There are New Testament churches today because Paul and the apostles believed in a follow-up discipleship program.

Outstanding missionaries constantly train new converts to be soulwinners. Christian begetting Christian was the way the early church grew, people going from house to house preaching and teaching the Word of God (Acts 20:20-21). Modern Christianity has the idea that a church building or its program and activities will draw people to Jesus Christ, but the Bible teaches that people are drawn when Christians go out into the highways and hedges and compel them to come to Jesus Christ. Even with gospel teams winning souls to the Lord in meetings, a follow-up and discipleship program is necessary to conserve the results. The young people on the gospel teams will be disappointed if they do not see their efforts producing changed lives. The principle of II Timothy 2:2 can help produce those results.

Evangelism and soulwinning is not the only emphasis necessary for a vital youth group, but it is a giant key to motivating teen-agers for Jesus Christ and getting them on the path of full-time service and giving them a cause to which they will rally.

Of course, before the leader can have a proper evangelism program in his group, he must be fully involved himself. Teen-agers will seldom go further than the leader has gone. If he does not invite others out to church, if he does not pass out tracts, if he does not witness and lead souls to Jesus Christ, if he does not disciple them, then it is going to be very difficult to get the teens motivated and excited about soulwinning. The leader has to be the one who gets it started and demonstrates how it is done. The youth group's soulwinning zeal will begin to spread to the whole church. Many a soulwinning church has started with a zealous soulwinning youth director inspiring the youth to get on fire for God.

A godly youth leader sees the tremendous need and potential of the youth for evangelism and gets them training others to win souls to Jesus Christ to pass on this heritage. This is how souls have been saved down through time. In the last fifty years, literally thousands upon thousands of souls have been affected by the people who were won by Bob Jones, Sr., Percy Crawford, Dawson Trotman, John R. Rice, and many others who then trained men to be soulwinners. Evangelism will help motivate teens to carry out the great commission for the rest of their lives and will build a superior youth program.

---

[1] Dawson Trotman first put this idea into practice in 1935, as explained in his booklet *Born to Reproduce,* published by Back to the Bible.

[2] Write to Minutemen Evangelistic Outreach, Bob Jones University, Greenville SC 29614.

Chapter 11
Counseling:
Listening and Confronting

A counseling ministry is an important part of the youth worker's responsibility. The goal of counseling is adjustment: to God and His will, to others, to self, and to circumstances. During the adolescent period the teen has certain specific adjustments to make as he goes from childhood to adulthood:

1. Accepting his physical development and sex role
2. Controlling his emotions
3. Being socially accepted
4. Finding his identity as a uniquely created person
5. Becoming independent and making choices, while still respecting authority and seeking wise counsel
6. Gaining financial responsibility
7. Establishing his character
8. Learning to set goals
9. Developing positive faith attitudes and eliminating negative devil attitudes
10. Learning to love people and touch other lives for God
11. Assuming the unselfish attitude of a servant
12. Developing his own moral and spiritual values.

Parents have the main responsibility for counseling their teen-age son or daughter, and most parents will be a real asset as they help their teen make adjustments in his life. They know their teen better than anyone else, and most parents are well aware of his strengths, weaknesses, problems, and difficulties. However, some parents are not good counselors because they have not solved their own problems. They let their own difficulties, frustrations, and reactions cloud their discernment and judgment in handling their teen's problems. Many times the teen's problems are just a reflection of the parents' unsolved problems.

Qualities of a Good Counselor

The youth leader becomes a confidant to most of the teens at one time or another because of his close contact with them. He is in a unique position to be a help both to the teens and their families. A good youth leader, however, may be hesitant to counsel, fearing that without training in psychology he may give bad advice or even cause psychological damage to the teens.

What qualities does a leader need to become a good counselor for teens? The first requirement is to be a well-adjusted person who has solved his own problems and is spiritually minded. The second requirement is a thorough knowledge of Bible principles and their applications to everyday problems. Third is a loving, accepting, listening spirit. Fourth is the wisdom to discover sinful behavior and teach the teen-ager the steps needed to bring his attitudes and behavior back into line with God's Word. A youth leader armed with the principles of the Word of God can give teens and their families a fresh, objective viewpoint, solid Biblical directions, and wise counsel.

Models of Mental Problems

In trying to determine the basic cause of psychological problems, Sigmund Freud came to some conclusions which have been called the "Medical Model": mental problems are labeled as an illness or sick behavior. According to Freud, the person is not responsible for the societal, familial, and environmental influences that caused his mental illness.

Furthermore, only a qualified psychiatrist or therapist can give proper treatment, which consists largely of ventilating feelings.

In his book *The Crisis in Psychiatry and Religion,* O. H. Mowrer, former president of the American Psychological Association, rejects the Medical Model of Freud and proposes the "Moral Model": problems are caused by guilt, which results from a person's violating his own moral standards (not necessarily God's standards). The person himself, then, is responsible for his behavior and can cure himself by confessing his sin (to anyone) and changing his behavior.

Christian counselors reject both of these models, adhering instead to the Scriptural "Spirit-Flesh Model" (Galatians 5:17-26; see Table IX); problems are caused by guilt, which results from sinful attitudes and behavior in direct violation of God's standards in His Word.

All people, Christians included, have the flesh—or self-focus—within them, warring against the Spirit. The Christian counselor asserts that the person bears sole responsibility for his problems, because he has given in to the flesh and sinned by going against God's laws and will (James 1:14). God can restore a repentant man who makes up his mind to confess his sin to Christ and to trust Him for complete forgiveness. The person must then crucify self daily (Luke 9:23) and go God's direction if he is to be well adjusted.

Jesus Christ conquered the devil, death, and the sin nature at the cross. Because of that victory, the flesh does not have a stranglehold grip over Christians (Romans 6). The believer must make up his mind in the power of Christ to walk in the Spirit (Galatians 5:24-25) and not to make provision for the flesh, to fulfill its lusts (Romans 13:14).

This model does not supply easy answers to some cases in which the problems are foregone results of sin's consequences (Exodus 20:5); cases in which a sovereign God is working His perfect will in a life (Job 23:10); or some cases of demon possession, which must be treated in a different way (Mark 9:29).

TABLE IX
SPIRIT-FLESH MODEL
THE BATTLE WITHIN

SERVE SIN — FLESH					SERVE RIGHTEOUSNESS — SPIRIT					
0	1	2	3	4	5	6	7	8	9	10

False gospel - works — True gospel - faith, blood atonement of Christ

Feeling oriented - emotions (subjective) — Mind oriented - will (objective)

Rebellion against authority — Obedience to authority

Hate, Bitterness - revenge — Love - forgiveness

Lust - fornication — Purity - self-control, one flesh in marriage

Dissatisfaction - love of money — Peace - contentment

Pride - concern for self — Humility - concern for others

Unreality - entertainment, TV, unwholesome fiction — Reality - servanthood, loving people

Sensual music - rhythm — Uplifting music - melody, harmony, balance

Temporal high - drugs, alcohol — Joy in the Lord - praise

WHICH DIRECTION?
Rev. 3:15-16
Gal. 5:24
Rom. 6:11-13; 7:15-25
James 1:8

SIN
Worldliness
(Rom. 13:14)
Self reigns
(Gal. 5:19-21)

HOLINESS
Complete dedication
(Rom. 12:1-2)
Self is crucified
(Gal. 2:20; 5:22-24;
Luke 9:23)

Pastors and Christians who thoroughly know the Word of God are best qualified to be counselors for those with mental problems. If the mental problem is caused by physical difficulties, the person should be referred to a physician.

Major Causes of Mental Problems

When a counselor deals with the problems of teens, he finds some basic causes. One youth director said that the troubled teens he deals with are either bad, sad, or mad, and his job is to make them glad. This may sound oversimplified, but Hebrews 12:15-16 similarly indicates three types of basic problems: "Looking diligently lest any man fail of the grace of God; lest any root of bitterness springing up trouble you, and thereby many be defiled; Lest there be any fornicator, or profane person, as Esau, who for one morsel of meat sold his birthright."

Bitterness

One of the three given causes in these verses is the root of bitterness, which springs up against parents and others and begins to trouble the teen. A whole family or youth group is sometimes defiled by the teen-ager's rebellion and bitterness, which is in reality rebellion and bitterness against God. The forgiveness principle of Ephesians 4:30-32 is the cure for this problem.

Fornication

A second cause mentioned in this verse is fornication. This word covers all kinds of sex sins. It includes necking and petting; a habit of masturbation; pornography; incest with brothers, sisters, relatives, or even parents; homosexuality; premarital sex; adultery; and various sexual perversions. The most common sin of fornication among teens is the habit of masturbation, occurring at some time in ninety-eight per cent of males' lives and about seventy-five per cent of females' lives, according to recent surveys. In the late teen years when young people are dating and going steady in unchaperoned situations, necking and petting are common sins. The tendency with those who practice these sins over a period of time is to get more intimate. Then the problems of premarital sex, pregnancy, abortion, and forced marriage begin to wreck their lives. The Bible indicates in I Corinthians 6:18 that fornication causes more physical and psychological problems than any other kind of sin: "Flee fornication. Every sin that a man doeth is without the body; but he that committeth fornication sinneth against his own body."

Christian psychologists, pastors, and counselors know that people with terrible guilt feelings, severe psychological problems, or psychosomatic diseases usually are involved or have been involved in some sex sin. The purity principle as found in I Thessalonians 4:1-7 is a help in dealing with the sins of fornication.

Another help is the three-point formula of Romans 14:17, useful for getting rid of gross sins that are wrecking the life: "For the kingdom of God is not meat and drink; but righteousness, and peace, and joy in the Holy Ghost." First, righteousness comes by taking full responsibility for the sin instead of trying to blame another for it, and by confessing it before God (Isaiah 1:18; Ephesians 1:7; I John 1:7). Second, peace comes by forgetting the sin after it has been cleansed (Philippians 3:13; Isaiah 43:18-19, 25). Third, joy in the Holy Ghost comes by praising God for His forgiveness (Isaiah 44:22-23; Psalm 107:8).

Materialism

Finally, Hebrews 12:15-16 shows us a third main cause of problems: a materialistic, worldly viewpoint, which results in profane, feeling-oriented, pleasure-mad, Epicurean behavior, leaving God out. Teens that are hooked on rock music, drugs, sports, and flashy cars have the worldly viewpoint. They are in the fast lane, and sensual pleasure and money are more important than God's standards, self-respect, or their testimony for Christ. Rebellion and discontentment are symptoms of this viewpoint. An understanding of the kingdom-of-God principle as found in Matthew 6:19-34 and the contentment principle found in I Timothy 6:6-10 is helpful for dealing with materialism and worldliness.

Other Causes of Mental Problems

These three causes given in Hebrews 12:15-16 seem to underlie most teen problems. But there are three other basic causes of problems.

Rejection

One is negative rejection feelings, which are usually based on selfishness. Most people feel rejected at one time or another in their lives, beginning in childhood and peaking in the teen years. About thirty per cent of all girls feel so rejected that at some time in their childhood they imagine that they are adopted. As teens are rebuffed at home, in school, and in social and dating situations, they begin to feel that everyone is looking down on them and is against them. They become sensitive to the cuts, slights, and snide remarks of their parents, friends, and authority figures. They feel socially, and therefore emotionally, rejected by others.

Appearance, intelligence, physical abilities, and the family's socio-economic status (in that order) have the greatest effect on a teen's feeling of rejection. Physical handicaps and poor home life can also have an adverse effect. As these rejection feelings grow, some teen-agers begin to set up their defenses and to withdraw into a selfish, self-centered, introspective existence that produces personality abnormalities and disturbances, sometimes resulting in suicide.

Since 1970 teen suicides have increased at an alarming rate. Each year, approximately 2,000,000 teen-agers attempt suicide, and 6,000 teen-agers succeed. Some experts believe the primary cause of suicide is the lack of a meaningful relationship with at least one parent. A Penn State study found that the average parent spends less than seven minutes per week in intense personal time with his child. Charles Solomon in his books, *The Rejection Syndrome* and *The Handbook to Happiness,* deals with this problem and suggests

Ephesians 1:6-7 as a cure for the problem: "To the praise of the glory of his grace, wherein he hath made us accepted in the beloved. In whom we have redemption through his blood, the forgiveness of sins, according to the riches of his grace."

He believes that rejection is the basic problem of most people, even born-again Christians. The basis of all rejection feelings, he says, is the person's belief that he is not accepted by God because of his sins. God through Jesus Christ and His shed blood completely accepts the believer. "There is therefore now no condemnation to them which are in Christ Jesus, who walk not after the flesh, but after the Spirit" (Romans 8:1). God has made the Christian "accepted in the beloved," Jesus Christ, and He takes away all condemnation. He holds the Christian in His hand and completely accepts him into His family (I John 3:1). If Christians are accepted by God, they no longer need worry about people's acceptance of them. Instead the Christian can deny self daily and start extending himself to others (Luke 9:23).

Fantasy-thinking

A fifth common cause of mental problems is humanistic fantasy-thinking (Romans 1:21). This attitude is man's reasoning about life's situations, giving little or no thought to God's control, His intervention, or His claims on the affairs of man. When situations develop or crucial events take place, the average man does not look to the principles of the Word of God for guidance in how he is to act and react. Instead, he constructs a pattern of thinking that is largely fantasy and involves his wishes, his sinful desires, unrealistic goals, and a make-believe world. This pattern of thinking is usually negative, for it goes against positive faith principles. When this fantasy thinking is acted out in real life, it results in tremendous difficulties. Television tends to accentuate the problem; the average person finds it hard to distinguish fantasy from God's reality after filling his brain with humanistic fantasy twenty-five to thirty hours a week. Many times this thinking is a cover-up for guilt feelings.

A principle used to deal with this cause is twofold. The negative aspect is found in II Corinthians 10:5: "Casting down imaginations, and every high thing that exalteth itself against the knowledge of God, and bringing into captivity every thought to the obedience of Christ." The positive aspect is portrayed in Philippians 4:8: "Finally, brethren, whatsoever things are true, whatsoever things are honest, whatsoever things are just, whatsoever things are pure, whatsoever things are lovely, whatsoever things are of good report; if there be any virtue, and if there be any praise, think on these things."

For example, the person struggling with fantasy can make a list of good things that have happened or good things he can plan and do. Then when bad thoughts come, he can pull out this list and have some definite good thoughts as replacements for the bad. He must make up his mind to cast down any imaginings incompatible with the knowledge of God and think positive faith thoughts. Negative fantasy thinking is the most common reason for a Christian's giving in to temptation: "A good man out of the good treasure of the heart bringeth forth good things: and an evil man out of the evil treasure bringeth forth evil things" (Matthew 12:35).

Physical causes

Finally, there are physical causes for many severe problems. A blow on the head or a brain tumor will obviously injure the brain and affect behavior. However, more subtle physical problems, such as allergies, hormone cycles, drugs, anemia, vitamin deficiencies, fatigue, upset blood sugar levels, spirochetes, and viruses can seriously affect a person's actions and reactions. When a counselor suspects a physical problem because the person does not respond to counseling, he should suggest that the person see a medical doctor for a check-up.

Non-medical suggestions to alleviate the physical symptoms might include getting regular exercise, decreasing consumption of sweets, getting adequate protein, taking daily vitamins with iron, getting proper sleep (women on the average need more than men), keeping regular hours, and setting aside relaxing "Praise the Lord" times during the day. Girls should be aware of their normal hormone cycles, which can cause two or three depressed and moody episodes in a month's time.

Strategy for Solving Problems

Once the counselor is aware of the various causes of problems, he can then help the teen by being first a detective (finding the root cause by listening for clues) and then a teacher (equipping the teen with Bible principles that he can use to solve his problem).

As a **detective,** the counselor *asks questions* and gives careful attention to the answers, letting the Holy Spirit guide in handling the information. His goal is to help the teen solve his own problems. Some of the questions that the counselor may ask to discover the problems and root causes follow.

1. How do you feel toward your mother, father, brothers, and sisters?
2. What do you feel guilty about?
3. What is your biggest area of temptation?
4. What makes you very angry?
5. What is your biggest problem?
6. What would you change about yourself if you could?
7. What makes you fearful and afraid?
8. What are your goals in life?
9. Who would you want to be if you had a choice?
10. What makes you feel very rejected?
11. What do you think is your greatest need?

After asking pertinent questions, the counselor *listens* until the Holy Spirit helps him discern the problem that is upsetting the teen and causing him to become confused, depressed, angry, or rebellious against God. The process is like putting a jigsaw puzzle together. When there are an adequate number of pieces in place, the counselor gets some idea of what the whole picture is about.

After finding the root cause or causes, a good counselor becomes a **teacher,** *pointing out* the Bible principles and the steps which the person needs to take to eliminate the cause and solve his problem. He also *motivates* the counselee to work toward the solution, but it is up to the individual to choose to go God's way or to continue in his sinful direction. In the next interview, the counselor should ask the counselee what steps he has taken to solve his problems.

Principles for Counselors

Besides imparting Bible principles, counselors must themselves follow some basic principles in detecting problems and helping teens solve them.

Finding the sin

One of the first principles that good counselors follow is this: look for the sin that is behind most severe problems. Sin, with the resulting guilt feelings and fear of judgment, causes people to have emotional and physical breakdowns and to end up in mental hospitals. Jay E. Adams, after working with patients in two mental hospitals, is convinced that most patients are there not because they are sick but because they are sinful. In his book *Competent to Counsel,* he challenges Christians to help people with severe problems by confronting them with their sin, teaching them to confess it and to follow Bible principles.

O. H. Mowrer (author of the Moral Model), though he does not claim to be a born-again Christian, also attacks the idea that mental problems are illnesses. He says instead that they are due to a violated conscience, with the resulting guilt feelings that can drive a person insane.

In his book *Whatever Became of Sin?* Karl Menninger makes the point that modern psychiatry has explained away sin by redefining it as sickness caused by early childhood influences. If one is sick, then he is not responsible for his "symptomatic" actions, so the thinking goes. Although sinful behavior is usually the result of a deeper sin problem, calling it a "symptom" and implying that the root cause is a sickness hinders the person from taking full responsibility for his sin and confessing it; furthermore, superficial treatment of the "symptoms" may result in even more severe problems.

Christian counselors need to confront the person with his sin and help him to acknowledge it, take full responsibility for it, confess it, and then go God's way to keep from further sin. This is the real solution to most of the difficult problems causing emotional upsets.

Using the Word

A second principle is to use the Word of God to detect and solve people's problems. Hebrews 4:12 assures the youth leader that the Bible is the best counseling tool he could possibly use. Hence, a good counselor knows the Scriptures thoroughly and is able to apply the appropriate verses to the problems with which he deals. There is not a problem in life that the Bible does not deal with at least in principle. The thirty-seven Bible principles given in Appendix A are useful principles in the solution of the common problems. The 4-M Formula (see Appendix A) can be beneficial in helping the teen to apply Bible principles. One of the goals of counseling is to increase the teen's faith in God, and "faith cometh by hearing, and hearing by the word of God"(Romans 10:17).

Directing the counselee

Third, the counselor should have the counselee do something. After a counseling session, the counselee should have a definite plan of action for solving his problem: for instance, he can jog, read certain passages of Scripture, apologize and ask forgiveness of the hated one, destroy his rock music collection, praise the Lord for five minutes twice a day, set goals for victory over a habit, memorize certain Scriptures, or take other steps that are appropriate to the solution of the problem. It is not what the counselor does but what the counselee does about his problem that starts him toward the solution.

The counselor should give two or three steps and have the counselee write them down. Then the counselor should carefully explain and illustrate each step. At the next session he should follow up on these activities and their results to see whether progress has been made.

Basic Counseling Truths

Knowledge of several basic truths can be of help to the counselor. The first is that **time solves many problems,** especially in cases of depression. Therefore, encouraging the teen through the few days beyond the situation or the stress of the moment usually minimizes the problem to the point where the teen can handle it adequately. By that time, in many cases, the problem may even cease to exist. Some girls at certain points in their hormone cycles enlarge the ordinary problems of teen years into critical episodes. Waiting three or four days to handle the problem often improves their whole outlook. Parents and friends also may change their attitudes and behavior over a period of time, thus improving the teen's response. Nevertheless, teens still need to acquire techniques of using Bible principles to handle their everyday problems so that these problems no longer become critical. The following principles are particularly helpful.

1. Give thanks in everything (Ephesians 5:20; Philippians 4:6; I Thessalonians 5:18).
2. Be content with the situation into which God has put you (Philippians 4:11; I Timothy 6:6).
3. Be angry at sin, but do not sin in anger (Ephesians 4:26-27).
4. Express love instead of vengeance (Romans 12:19-21).
5. Control your thoughts (II Corinthians 10:5; Philippians 4:8).
6. Confess sin immediately (I John 1:9).
7. Resist the devil, and flee from temptation (I Corinthians 10:13; I Peter 5:8; James 4:7).

Second, **anger or guilt is usually the cause of depression,** the most common mental problem. Depression here means a vague, heavy feeling of melancholy preventing one from being able to cope with ordinary responsibilities. Bottled-up anger that has been allowed to fester over a period of time turns inward upon the person himself, causing depression; it is a short-circuiting of one's dynamic energies. Guilt feelings, which arouse fears of judgment, also bring on depression.

Physical problems can also contribute to depression. Women become depressed much more frequently than men and are very much affected by their normal hormone cycles.[1] Beginning regular jogging or other aerobic exercise, decreasing the sugar intake, and ensuring good nutrition and rest can often not only cure depression but also eliminate certain frustrations and prevent some sin problems from arising.

Third, **sex sins have the most damaging effects** on the body and the mind. I Corinthians 6:18 suggests this idea. Homosexuality, which is against a person's very nature, causes more personality problems than any other sin. Medical experts agree that homosexuality is not a physiological problem (i.e., due to hormone imbalance or some other purely physical development) except in very rare cases of hermaphroditism; rather, it is a psychological problem (i.e., due to deliberate decisions by the individual).

Many ideas have been suggested for the cause for these wrong decisions. Of course, continual remarks about a child's appearance, actions, or mannerisms being like those of the opposite sex can cause him to be confused about his sex orientation. But the most common factor in the background of homosexuals is a home that contains a domineering, over-protective mother and a weak, ineffectual, or absent father. A related problem is a home with no proper role model of the same sex while the child is between the ages of three and fourteen. Divorced or widowed women must make sure that their boys have good father-substitutes during these years.

Another motivating factor is the "first pleasure" principle. A boy between the ages of six and fifteen who experiences extreme sex pleasure with another boy will tend to repeat this first sex pleasure experience in later years. Then he will begin to wonder if he is not destined to be locked into a gay lifestyle because of his strong desire for this kind of pleasure. With girls, who are touch-oriented, this tendency can start with other girls through innocent back massages that develop into sensuous erotic pleasure, bringing all kinds of doubts about their sex orientation. But regardless of what influenced the person toward his wrong decisions, homosexuality is still a matter of sinful choices, not an inevitable destiny.

The habits of masturbation, necking and petting, voyeurism, pornography, and transvestism, if indulged in during preteen years, may carry over into the teen years and cause tremendous psychological problems. The same kinds of habits starting in teen years can cause severe guilt feelings, especially in girls, who seem to have a more tender consciences toward these sins than boys.

A study by Dr. Seymour Hallack at the University of Wisconsin Psychiatric Clinic of 103 girls with severe psychiatric problems found that eighty-seven per cent were regularly committing fornication with at least one man and seventy-three per cent of them were sinning with two or more men. This study indicates why a counselor can conclude that sex sins are a root cause of many psychological problems.

Fourth, **sin habits can be broken and eliminated from one's life.** Soul erosion is much like soil erosion. Just a little sin, which becomes a habit and then develops into deeper sin, can cause many severe problems. A person at any point in time can decide to turn from his wicked sin habits, get complete forgiveness, and start following God's plain principles for his actions. First of all, he must recognize his habit as sin and genuinely confess it (I John 1:9). Next, he must set a definite time goal for victory (for instance, three days, then three weeks, then three months), until finally the habit is no longer a temptation (I Corinthians 10:13). Every time the temptation arises, he should get some kind of physical exercise to sublimate or redirect his energies into other channels. In addition, an appropriate scripture verse, praise, and prayer will help in times of extreme temptation.

Fifth, **double-mindedness causes instability, indecisiveness, and confusion.** James 1:8 states that "a double minded man is unstable in all his ways." Teens must learn how to make decisions, because when they waver between two or more opinions, they tend to get confused. The steps for solid decision making follow.

1. Determine what the choices are.
2. Find out when a decision must be made.
3. Get all the information needed.
4. See what the Bible says about it.
5. Pray for wisdom and for God to change the circumstance if it is His will.
6. Act on the decision that has been made.

Men in particular need to learn to be decisive, since decision making is the heart of leadership, and spiritual leadership is the God-given responsibility of the man.

Sixth, **rebellion against authority, coupled with discontent, causes problems in many areas of life.** The authority principle is a crucial guide that must be first learned in childhood and adhered to throughout life if a person is to experience God's blessing. The average teen desiring independence from family authority may get into the habit of rebellion against authority in general. Rebellious teens become insecure and discontented (I Timothy 6:1-6). Parents can help their teens by gradually relaxing control and giving them more opportunities for choices and decisions.

Seventh, **wild and corrupt thoughts must be controlled.** Everyone has crazy thoughts at times. A man might be on the twentieth-story balcony of a Hyatt Regency hotel looking down on the people dining or milling about in the lobby below and have the crazy idea to spit, drop a plastic bag filled with water, or even jump and commit suicide. He immediately determines that it is a crazy thought, perhaps even put there by the devil, who can have access to the mind. A rational Christian does not dwell on these wild thoughts but rather learns to cast these thoughts out of his mind and refuses to think about them (II Corinthians 10:5). He replaces them with right thoughts, according to Philippians 4:8. This simple procedure must be followed also with all corrupt thoughts.

Eighth, **dreams should not be interpreted.** Dreams are God's method of cleaning out the corruption and useless material from the brain. God also uses dreams as a sex release for both men and women. Thus, a person who does not dream can have mental problems.

One usually dreams five dreams a night, about twenty minutes per dream, but does not remember the dreams unless he awakens during them and recalls the details within the first ten minutes. God does not want dreams (the useless material) reprogrammed into the brain.

Ninth, **the servant attitude is basic** to a well-adjusted life of service for the Lord (Phil. 2:5-8). Following Christ's example of servanthood is a prerequisite for doing the Lord's work effectively. There is no limit to what can be accomplished if a person is willing to follow the Lord's leadership and give Him the credit. Being humble enough to do the menial tasks and take the low place puts the Christian in the position to be greatly used of the Lord.

Other Kinds of Counseling

In addition to counseling for personal problems, the youth leader will be doing a great deal of educational counseling, which is a basis for vocational counseling. If he can get his high school graduates into a good Christian Bible college or university, he has the educational and vocational battle pretty well won. Experts there can advise a student about his major and his vocational choices.

Many parents tend to think in terms of a community college, believing that with their child living at home, protected from the corruption of the world, they will better be able to foster their young person's Christian growth. However, this idea works against what should be the ultimate goal of every Christian parent: to make their child an independent adult, able to cope with the real world and get the skills and training necessary to succeed as a servant of God.

Students do need a wholesome educational environment in which the influence for Christian service predominates. They also need to come in contact with other Christian men and women, to develop lifelong friendships and to find a marriage partner. A Christian college can meet these needs, provided that it is known for its high standards of Christian conduct as well as its opportunity for student development physically, emotionally, intellectually, socially, culturally, and spiritually. A youth leader can help his teens choose the right school for them.

The choice of a Christian college or university is best made after students have visited one or more of them. The youth leader, then, should set up college tours of several campuses. Most colleges have "college days" or "get acquainted days" or special holiday times when visiting high school students can come and even stay in the dormitories. These kinds of visits can be productive in getting students started in the right direction for their Christian calling and vocation.

Counseling youth can be a rewarding use of the youth leader's time. If he is directed by the Holy Spirit in his counseling, he can see eternal results from these individual contacts. A dedicated heart of love and a sincere interest in the teens' welfare are indispensable ingredients for helping a young person.

---

[1] This source of depression is discussed at length in Chapter 16 of *Formula for Family Unity*.

Chapter 12
Demonstrating and Training Leadership: "Which Way Did They Go? I'm Their Leader!"

The youth leader must train teens to be leaders if he hopes to produce a generation of dynamic Christians who will make an impact on their world. The youth leader has under his influence a great pool of potential Christian leaders. The training he gives them in leadership can make a significant difference in the leadership of the church in future years.

The Need for Godly Leadership

Leadership is vital for success. Important endeavors do not just happen. Someone has an idea and takes the initiative to make it happen. When two or more people form a group, someone dominates—someone eventually becomes the leader. There are two kinds of leaders: natural leaders and appointed leaders. Natural leaders usually become the appointed leaders. Though appointed leaders may not always know much about leadership, they can learn good leadership principles and become successful leaders.

God, in His Word, appoints certain leaders: a pastor over a church, parents over their children, and rulers over people. However, leadership is a function and not a position. God-appointed leaders may or may not show leadership; but if they do not, some kind of leadership will emerge in the group.

That emerging leadership will often be negative leadership, taking the group away from its set goals. For example, if a father will not show leadership in the home, then the wife or sometimes a rebellious teen will assume leadership. If the youth leader will not lead, then someone in the group will emerge as the leader—perhaps a dynamic worldly teen, or the wife of the couple who are helping him as sponsors. If this emerging leadership is negative, or opposed to the goals he has set for the group, then much dissension, grief, and trouble result. Therefore, the Christian leader (the position) must have a firm grasp on leadership (the function) in order to get anything accomplished for God.

The Definition of Godly Leadership

Christian leadership may be defined as motivating others to want and accomplish the same God-glorifying goals that the leader has for the group. This definition requires that the competent youth leader have a sound philosophy of youth work, proper goals, and a knowledge of the principles of leadership that will motivate people to want to reach those goals.

Proper goals are **attainable.** Even the best group will become discouraged if its goals are unrealistic. But there is great satisfaction for an individual or a group when they reach their goals. Proverbs 13:12 and 19 state, "Hope deferred maketh the heart sick, but when the desire cometh it is a tree of life. . . . The desire accomplished is sweet to the soul."

The goals must also be financially **feasible.** Since the budget of Christian groups is usually small, goals should take into account the money available. In addition, goals should be in line with the philosophy and purpose of both the organization and the Word of God.

Finally, goals should be **both long-range and immediate.** Long-range goals are good for overall planning, but they must be broken down into immediate goals to get the best response from a group.

To train young people properly, the leader needs to concentrate on developing their leadership skills. This training involves more than just teaching the qualities of leadership; it also means giving the teens opportunities to develop their leadership skills in actual situations. Delegating responsibilities and guiding the teens through the successful completion of a project help them to gain confidence and motivate them to take on more leadership tasks.

The Qualities of Godly Leadership

The qualities of Christian leadership can be examined from three different viewpoints: (1) What are the leader's personal characteristics? (2) What does he do in leading? (3) What are the characteristics and attitudes of the group that is being led?

Personal characteristics

The lists may differ, but most studies agree on certain personal traits found in most outstanding leaders.

Decisiveness is crucial, since decision making is the heart of leadership. Leaders generally learn to make decisions early in life, but overprotected children with authoritarian parents have few opportunities to learn how to make decisions and live with the consequences. To develop this trait in teens, the youth leader should give them opportunities to make decisions, let them enjoy the fruits of good decisions, and encourage them to learn from poor decisions. For example, let the teens plan the banquet or the recreation program for the camp. If it succeeds in grand style, they get the credit. If it bombs, they count it a lesson learned for planning future events.

Good communication skills are vital for leaders. Leaders must listen, get ideas, and then be able to organize the best points and present them for their followers' understanding. Training in this area can come in an idea-sharing time with teens. Get each participant to present his summation and his plan gleaned from the discussion.

147

Character is essential, for people will follow leaders who are consistent and dependable, those who operate on principle instead of impulses and feelings of the moment. The youth leader should constantly teach teens Bible principles and how to apply them consistently. Teens must learn to discipline various areas of their lives and bring their desires under the control of the Spirit-filled mind. For example, their desire for sensual behavior on dates must be governed by the purity principle.

Enthusiasm is important for a leader. It requires a positive faith attitude and dynamic energy properly directed. Most teens tend to be negative and fearful, and they must be trained to use, by faith, God's power that is within them to do His will. Teens can learn that God will always work something out to help them solve the problem. This knowledge will motivate them to do things "heartily as unto the Lord" (Colossians 3:23). A teen needs to be trained to walk briskly wherever he goes and to be enthusiastic about the things at hand. When talking to someone, he should learn to look the person in the eye and talk purposefully instead of mumbling with a hang-dog look. A fresh, vibrant attitude is the result of an enthusiastic approach to life.

Knowledge, which is often quite separate from superior intelligence, is valuable for leaders. It helps them to take an interest in reading and in acquiring the perspective essential for decision making. Teens need to be in the habit of having a regular input of knowledge from the Bible, good books, magazines, and tapes. Such learning both gives them a broad foundation for Christian leadership and stimulates the imagination they need for planning and setting goals.

Love, resulting in warm relationships with others, is essential for the superior leader. This love is built on a servant's attitude, thinking of others and being willing to make sacrifices of time, energy, and money. Mutual trust, respect, and good communication build strong friendships upon which love is based. Teens can develop this attitude by deferring to the wishes of others, listening, and being aware of one another's problems and successes.

Actions

Leaders do certain things to manifest leadership. Among them are the following.

Planning Leaders are goal-oriented, and they develop plans for achieving their goals. Teens should be taught to set daily and weekly goals, writing down everything they have to do, numbering the goals in order of importance, and then accomplishing them. The leader can have "brainstorming" planning sessions with the teens and then help them to boil these ideas down into realistic and workable plans. In planning, leaders must acknowledge God (Proverbs 3:5-6) and commit their work to the Lord so that He can establish their thoughts (Proverbs 16:3). Then they can be assured that He will direct their planning (Proverbs 16:9).

Deciding Leaders accept problems as challenges that need creative decisions. They are willing to take the responsibility of deciding and are willing to live with the consequences. They do not wait for things to happen; they cause things to happen by deciding and then continually explaining what is happening. The steps of decision making involve answering these questions:

1. What choices do I have?
2. How much time do I have to decide?
3. What Bible principles apply?
4. What information do I need?
5. What kind of decision and action is necessary?

Teens need to be encouraged to ask all kinds of questions before making a decision. After they make the decision, they should take positive action rather than engaging in negative questioning about the feasibility of the decision. The youth leader should teach teens to make up their minds, using the example of Joshua as an outstanding, decisive leader (Joshua 24:15).

Delegating It is not what one does but what one gets done that really counts. The teens or lay leaders should do most of the work that takes up the youth leader's time, and they in turn can learn to delegate some of their work. Successful delegation requires human relationships built on good communication, friendship, and respect. Knowing the strengths and weaknesses of people helps the leader to delegate the right tasks to the right people as he uses people's strengths. Teens can be trained not to care who gets the credit but to find their satisfaction in seeing great things accomplished for God.

Moses' father-in-law taught him how to delegate so that he could endure the overwhelming task and not wear away (Exodus 18:14-27). The greatest failure of Christian leaders is trying to do everything themselves. Since appropriate delegation multiplies leadership potential, the good leader leads best by reproducing himself.

Organizing A group must have patterns of organization, standard operating procedures, and well-defined roles for each member of the group. The Bible commands Christians to do things decently and in order (I Corinthians 14:40). First, the youth leader must motivate teens and rally support for the goals and for the plans to achieve them. Next, he must break down a big project into small, practical steps and immediately attainable objectives. Finally, he can give the officers or teen council a continual part in organizing so that they see great things being accomplished for God. Supplies should also be organized as well. There should be a place for everything and everything in its place. "Put it back" is the rule if the youth group wants to have supplies on hand for its activities.

Supervising Youth leaders inspect what they expect. Even though they have delegated the authority, they cannot delegate the responsibility. The responsibility is the leader's to make sure the task is done in the right way and at the right time. Teens easily get off the main trail, and keeping them headed toward the goal is part of good supervision. Positive reinforcement, encouragement, and help in solving problems will counteract the typical teen's tendency to give up or to cancel the activity. *The good leader never cancels an activity,* for a leader can always solve the problem somehow with God's help, by using some imagination and by being flexible. For example, the group whose plans to go snow skiing are spoiled by a four-day rainy spell may have to go 150 miles farther north (adding an overnight stay). If that is not possible, they might go to the city's indoor ice-skating rink, or the leader may even change the activity completely to a bowling party or a museum trip with a meal at a Chinese restaurant.

Teens can learn to supervise and exhibit a great sense of responsibility if given the proper training. One of the best examples of a leader's initiating the steps of leadership is found in the book of Nehemiah. Nehemiah planned with much prayer (chapters 1 and 2), made his decision (chapter 2, verses 17 and 20), delegated (chapter 3), organized (chapter 4), and supervised (chapters 5 and 6). The great task of rebuilding the walls of Jerusalem was accomplished in just fifty-two days through a human leader wholly dedicated to God.

The Objective of the Godly Leader

Though the purpose of the church and youth group is evangelism and the goals toward that purpose are many and varied, there is one main objective of the youth leader and every leader he grooms within the youth group: build healthy attitudes in others. Attitudes affect every aspect of the group, from its sense of identity (internal) to its ministry (external). Some of the vital attitude areas are as follows.

Discipline

A leader is well aware that the attitude of discipline must exist if the group is to function with any cohesiveness and effectiveness. He promotes discipline by having proper lines of authority and standard operating procedures for recurring situations (e.g., conducting a meeting, collecting money, serving refreshments, and transporting the teens home); the leader then has to handle only the exceptions.

On the other hand, when planning special events or making major decisions, a leader should not be bound by standard operating procedures. The leader should make his creative decisions and, when the plan is operational, establish his standard procedures for the routine tasks. For example, in planning a camping trip, he might decide to make it completely different from the one last year. Then the standard procedures for feeding and housing the group would have to be set up for that particular trip.

Morale

Esprit de corp is essential for a smoothly functioning group. The superior leader builds morale by promoting a team spirit. Nehemiah said, "Let *us* build up the wall. . . that *we* be no more a reproach. . . . Let *us* rise up and build. . . . They laughed *us* to scorn and despised *us*. . . . God . . . will prosper *us;* therefore *we* his servants will arise and build" (2:17).

Good communication helps morale. When the men were separated on the wall, Nehemiah used even the sound of the trumpet to maintain communication. A personal weekly contact with individuals helps them to feel important in the group. In addition, involving many teens in a project or activity makes them feel needed, knowing that their efforts contribute to success.

Morale depends on a sense of belonging and on love for one another. Teen leaders should be taught to take a personal interest in the spiritual welfare of every member of the group. Each leader should buddy up with some other teen, so that the two can check up weekly on each other regarding their spiritual responsibilities, such as soulwinning, devotions, and Bible memorization.

Dedication

The attitude of dedication to a cause (not to a human being) is crucial. The leader should always promote the cause. Leaders are human and have their weaknesses, and idealistic teens can be disappointed in individuals. The cause of Jesus

Christ, however, stands on the character of God and can never bring disappointment (Jeremiah 17:5-8). The leader's position must always be John 3:30: "He must increase, but I must decrease." As the leader lets God work in him "to will and to do of His good pleasure" (Philippians 2:13), the teens will have a living example of what it means to have Christ in control of a life. The cause of Jesus Christ lasts beyond the high school years and beyond any group or charismatic personalities. The worldwide compass of the gospel transcends provincial boundaries. The cause of Jesus Christ can best be promoted by emphasizing His holiness and His love for the lost and by making disciples of Christ.

Efficiency

The attitude of efficiency should permeate the actions of a dynamic group. A good leader is a student of time and motion efficiency and is always promoting the most efficient and best way to do things. Buying food wholesale, running kids down the food line on both sides of two tables rather than one side of one table, having every teen carry his chair to the wall, putting song books in a box on the way out, filling the separate cars or buses with kids from a certain section of town—these are all little but important ways of organizing to save time, money, and effort. Since money is in short supply in most Christian groups and since time is money, the leader must work toward getting goals accomplished with the least amount of either. It is God's will that "all things be done decently and in order" (I Corinthians 14:40). How an activity or project is organized will determine how efficiently it is carried out.

However, efficiency must always be balanced with class. A "bare bones" activity may save time and money, but it may need the extra touch of effort, money, and time to give it class or "pizzaz." Teens, like adults, respond to the first-class touch—the decorations, the paint job, the tablecloths, the dishes instead of paper plates at a banquet, the rented tour bus instead of the rickety school bus for the cross-country trip, and so on. Of course, these touches too must be within the budget. The leader is a scrounger, knowing where to beg, borrow, or get donations to spruce up the activity or program. For example, a big department store can lend certain theme decorations. Even though resources are limited, the desire should be to gain maximum benefit from both human and material resources.

Types of Leaders

A youth leader generally produces in his teens the kind of leadership that he himself exhibits. His leadership quality may be classified as one of three types of leaders: (1) positive, dynamic, creative leaders, (2) shoulder-shruggers, and (3) negative Neds.

Positive

The positive, dynamic leader has a well-thought-out philosophy, solid goals, character, and a positive faith attitude. He is always coming up with new ideas, has the youth's spiritual progress and welfare in mind, makes himself available to serve youth twenty-four hours a day, and works well under the authority of the pastor. The big danger for this type of leader is the neglect of his relationship with Christ and the neglect of wife and children. Such a leader can become a workaholic, working night and day to reach the goals he has set. He can also upset the conservative deacons and oldsters by his ambitious, creative plans and activities. The pastor, who has given full approval to his plans, may have to intercede for him. A balanced life with Bible convictions and a ministry of love helps the positive, dynamic leader to be a success and have a fruitful ministry, producing many full-time servants for God.

Neutral

The shoulder-shrugger is an easy-going person with few goals. He rarely gets excited about anything. He is available to the teens for counseling and as a resource person but gives little or no direction to the teens. This type of leader lets the teens do all the planning and execution of the activities and meetings. If there is a good teen leader in the group, that teen leader makes the group grow; otherwise, the group lumps along in the same old pattern week after week and begins to lose members. The shoulder-shrugger has no outreach; he is satisfied to work with the teens of the families of the church. If the church is growing, the group grows. If the church is on the decline, the shrugger does not realize that he may be part of the cause. Shoulder-shruggers are usually good Bible teachers, but they find only a small percentage of the teens responding in a life-changing way. This type of leader is a very loving person but rarely expresses his convictions, for he would not want to offend anyone.

Negative

A negative Ned is rebellious to authority in general. Because he does not get along with the pastor, he pulls against the pastor and perhaps the parents as well. He gets a few of the disgruntled parents on his side, then abets a split in the church. He tends to be dictatorial and legalistic, dwelling on some minor theme such as slacks, pierced ears, lipstick, dating, women not having leadership of any kind, or some other fad of the moment. He cuts back programs, and any suggestion from the teens or pastor "just won't work." The youth group suffers from his harsh attitudes and instability. He usually stays no longer than two or three years in any one church.

Principles of Motivation

Since motivation is such an important part of leadership, youth leaders should practice good principles of motivation. Although some of these principles apply primarily to the youth pastor, all can be incorporated to some degree into the lives of those teens that the youth pastor is training to be leaders themselves.

Highlighting the purpose

The leader must continually remind the teens of their main purpose—evangelism—as they put on their monthly activities. Teens should realize too that the youth activities are helping them as Christians to build character, to be equipped to do "the work of the ministry" (Ephesians 4:12), and to be conformed to the image of Christ (Romans 8:29).

Building communication

The youth leader must provide continual contact with the people he serves. He cannot be hidden away in an office. The teens, their parents, and other church members must know in which direction he is going and what is happening from week to week. The youth leader's plans and activities must have high visibility through church announcements in the bulletin and from the platform every Sunday night. The church members should be kept informed about not only what the youth will be doing but also what they have done. Also, the leader can communicate through staff meetings, parent meetings, individual conferences, and bi-monthly news bulletins containing the future calendar of events and other pertinent information.

The youth leader and the teens, of course, should be present and taking active part in the church's activities. Their participation helps to keep communication open. Good communication is built on understanding, so the superior leader continues explaining and making sure that he reaches all the people who should be aware of his program.

Ephesians 4:22-32 gives several rules for good communication. Verse 29 is the key: "Let no corrupt communication proceed out of your mouth, but that which is good to the use of edifying, that it may minister grace unto the hearers." That rule consistently applied guarantees superior communication in a group. Individuals must be edified by what is said and how it is said, including body language and facial expressions. The youth leader is aware of the persons who are responding, either accepting or rejecting what he is teaching or doing. He asks himself: "Do the teens feel accepted and loved or rejected by my actions toward them?" When the youth leader can communicate well, he is able to lead a group properly.

Using positive reinforcement

Teens want attention. They are so used to the negative attention received at home and school that they respond in a great way to positive attention. To have a disciplined group and maintain control, the youth leader must "reprove, rebuke [and] exhort with all longsuffering and doctrine" (II Timothy 4:2). Reproving and rebuking are usually negative and need to be balanced with exhortation or encouragement. The leader gives many compliments and acknowledgments, expressing much praise and appreciation both publicly and privately. He sandwiches needed criticisms between friendly words of greeting and recognition. This kind of positive reinforcement produces loyalty and a positive faith attitude within the group.

Proverbs 3:27, 12:25, 15:23, 16:24, and 25:11 explain what effect a good word at the right time can produce. People feel basically insecure and rejected; but the more support, acceptance, and appreciation that can be given the better people will be motivated and the more loyal they will become.

Subordinating things to people

Things wear out and are eventually discarded, but people live forever. Yet most leaders are better at managing things than people. A good leader continually studies how to manage people and is known as a people person. His concern and love for people in general and his followers in particular manifests itself in seeing that others are fed, housed, made comfortable, and having a good time before thinking of creature comforts for himself. Good leaders have an unselfish servant's attitude that soon permeates the whole group. The royal law of love (James 2:8) should become the standard for the youth group.

Taking responsibility

The leader is the problem solver. He should always have alternative actions ready. In emergencies he must trust the Lord to work things out, but he usually thinks ahead about what he might do in particular situations and makes adequate preparations. He seeks training to prepare himself to think and act in the right way—first aid, water safety instruction, CPR, leadership and counseling techniques, mechanics, and many other aids to help him to solve the problems that arise. When something or someone is not functioning, the leader must take the responsibility of seeing that the problem is handled properly. He can delegate authority and tasks, but he can't delegate responsibility. Responsibility always reverts upward to the leader and never downward to the follower.

Striving for excellence

Excellence is not perfection. All plans have their weaknesses and "bugs" that need to be worked out. The teens have their weaknesses and will never carry out plans perfectly. If the leader is a perfectionist, he will be disappointed in and critical of the teens for not properly producing and frustrated with things not working out the way he expected. Instead, the leader must work toward "bettering his best," "improving over last time," or showing "there is a better way." This improvement attitude will produce a spirit of excellence. Leaders plan to the best of their ability and expect to improve, modify, and adjust the application of these plans to people, circumstances, and situations, without sacrificing convictions or Bible principles.

Using legitimate techniques of persuasion

In many problem-solving situations, the leader needs to persuade others to his point of view. Morton Hunt[1] lists six techniques that he compiled from research studies on persuasion. First, use the home-turf advantage. The youth leader and the problem person should meet in the church office, the youth leader's home, or even a coffee shop rather than in the problem person's home. Second, look your best. People respond to a nice appearance as much as to what is said. Third, identify with your listeners. Hunt explains that the persuader should even "match the tone of voice, volume, rhythm and speech and even breathing patterns [of the other party], as most top salespeople have discovered." Fourth, reflect the listener's experience. The leader shows empathy and creates trust by first restating the other person's views and then giving his own before coming to a conclusion. Fifth, make a strong case. The leader does his homework and gets his facts together rather than giving opinions. He quotes good sources, research, and authorities to gain the other person's respect for his ideas. Sixth, employ stories and examples. A leader's own experiences are tremendous persuaders. These six techniques will help the leader to be a persuader in many confrontations.

Understanding the causes of behavior

There is a reason for the adverse reactions to plans, the bad feelings, the upset activities, and the tense human relationships. The leader must be willing to look first at his own actions and to accept the blame. What did he say wrong? Did he make a lousy decision? What was he not aware of? What did he forget? He should not act defensively or take personal offense but rather adjust the decision, make the apology, and do whatever is necessary to solve the problem and correct the situation.

He must continually seek to understand the motivations and behavior of himself and those he leads. He should always try to find the cause so that he can take the right steps of correction. Teens tend to be moody, up one week and down the next, and girls especially tend to be affected by their hormone cycles and by tense home situations. The need to be thought physically attractive to the opposite sex is another high priority with teens; it is part of the larger need to be noticed and given attention and appreciation. When efforts to fulfill a basic teen need such as this are continually thwarted, problems begin to arise. The cause of undesirable behavior, then, is not always immediately apparent. Yet rather than writing off the behavior as "just another phase they're going through," the good youth leader seeks to understand the needs, wants, and motivations of his teens.

Being flexible

Romans 8:14 says, "For as many as are led by the Spirit of God, they are the sons of God. " Leaders should continually let the Lord lead and direct the plans that they have prayed about. God's weather and God's plans never conflict; so when unexpected thunderstorms come on the day of the outdoor track and field day, leaders must make the adjustment. When the piano player or the lead tenor in the quartet ends up in the hospital from a car wreck while on the teen evangelistic music tour or when the youth leader's best lay assistant is transferred across the country, the leader gives thanks (I Thessalonians 4:18) and adjusts.

The youth leader also needs to make adjustments to people with their varying moods, their changing ideas or opinions, and their weaknesses and shortcomings. A good leader knows how to adapt within the framework of Bible principles. He wants God's plan for his life and for the group, and he must look to Him and to His Word continually for direction in every circumstance and contact.

Using these techniques of motivation will help a youth leader to exhibit effective leadership and to have success in training his teens to lead others in reaching God-glorifying goals.

Developing Leadership

Teens tend to follow leaders because they are so peer dominated. The wise youth leader uses competent teen leaders, those trained in leadership principles, to his advantage. As they learn the principles and get the practical experience in implementing the steps of leadership, these teens will be motivated to assume leadership positions in full-time Christian service.

In developing leaders within a group, the youth leader should start by picking members of a teen council who have the characteristics of leaders listed in this chapter. (There should be at least three council members for a youth group of thirty or fewer, and another council member for every ten youth group members above thirty.) The youth leader must make sure that the teens can conscientiously sign the youth council standards (given in Appendix E). He should try to have a representation of girls and boys of all ages, including all the minority groups and social levels that the church serves. From this council the youth group should elect officers (president, vice-president, secretary/treasurer, and others as needed).

The teen council should meet with the youth leader and his lay staff once a month for planning, challenge, motivation, and leadership training. Each teen council member should then contact his or her ten youth group members and "sell" the programs and activities, encouraging attendance and active participation. The council member can also squelch negative and rebellious attitudes and promote loyalty to the Word, to righteousness, and to their Lord and Saviour Jesus Christ.

All council members need to be used, even those not elected as officers. They can serve as committee chairmen or coordinators of special projects. Natural leaders will turn negative and sour if not used in some capacity. "Use me or lose me" is their unspoken cry.

Teens trained to be leaders will be better able to stand against the tyranny of peer domination (by which all are affected to a certain extent). Real leadership is learning to point oneself in God's way and then motivating others to go in the same direction. As teens learn to stand alone against peer pressure, they are also developing the courage they will need to stand against Satan and the temptations of the world.

Forming a New Generation

Proper leadership training helps the teen leader to grow in the Lord and will also make a big difference in the growth and development of the group as a whole.

---

[1] *Reader's Digest,* November 1983, p. 201.

Chapter 13
Building a Youth Group from Scratch:
Take It from Here

If a layman in a small church is asked to sponsor the youth group of only seven teens, where does he start? Or what does a pastor of a small new church do if he decides to implement something for the youth? What can workers do to build the youth group so that parents in the community will be attracted to the church because it has a good program for their teens? Starting a youth group or making a very small one grow can be a satisfying challenge if proven steps are followed.

Soulwinning Classes

The first step is to begin a soulwinning class to be held during the regular youth meeting time. The seven or eight teens in the youth group would all be members of the class. The youth leader can use the soulwinning training information in Chapter 10, giving the challenge, the five steps of evangelism, the survey techniques, and then practical assignments. The teens would learn the necessary soulwinning verses, view demonstrations, practice techniques in the class, and then go out to win their friends and use the follow-up procedures.

Teens often feel verbally incompetent and socially insecure. They need step-by-step instructions on what to say, how to respond, and what their actions should be.

The discipling of the converts they win is of utmost importance and can be the crucial factor in the success of the youth group's outreach program. Therefore the teen who wins the soul should do immediate follow-up by contacting the new convert at least once a week. During that contact he will answer questions, encourage the convert to memorize assurance and soulwinning verses, take him to church services and youth meetings, and get him to make a public profession with baptism. The teen should then take the new Christian soulwinning and have him give his testimony.

Public School Bible Clubs

As a second step, the youth leader should try to get a public high school Bible club going on Tuesday or Thursday morning before school or in the evening. The teens should meet at the house of one of the teens or at the leader's house. There they can be challenged with a soulwinning follow-up and prayer emphasis, learning what the teens in the youth group have already been instructed. The new converts in the club who are leaders should be singled out and taken under the direct tutelage of the youth leader, doing much of what Dawson Trotman did in the 1930s and 1940s with his clubs.[1] These public school Bible clubs will become feeders into the youth group and church and even the Christian school. A few of these teens might be lost to other churches, but if the churches are fundamentalist churches, the leader rejoices, for he is making an impact for Christ on the teens in his community. (See Appendix J.)

Evangelistic Meetings

The third step in developing a youth group would be holding a fresh, dynamic weekly evangelistic meeting for Christians, new converts, and sinners that have been invited to the meeting. This meeting could be held on a weeknight or on Sunday night. If it is held on Sunday night, a buffet supper should be served, with parents providing the food. This meeting should start with some peppy music, played by a good pianist and led by an enthusiastic song leader. It should be followed by several fresh testimonies from active teen soulwinners. These testimonies should include the funny situations and even the persecution which the teens have experienced. Testimonies of how Bible principles were put into action are also appropriate.

Then there must be a simple twenty-minute salvation message with an invitation. This type of message should be given week after week, with different Scriptures and illustrations. Very few people get saved on just one presentation of the gospel, and this constant review of salvation will also strengthen Christians, give them assurance, and provide them with illustrations for their soulwinning contacts. Other evangelists or youth speakers may occasionally be invited to give the message.

The message should be followed by a brief discussion of a topic pertinent to teens, such as dating, dress, issues of the day, news items, prophecy, or some Bible principle that would capture the attention of the teens.

The leader should obtain each visitor's name, address, telephone number, grade in high school, and other pertinent information. The youth leader can then match the visitor with a teen from the youth group who can follow up the initial contact and can be a friend to the visitor. Follow-up gives each teen soulwinning contacts, people that they will invite and even transport to future meetings and activities. The visitors will also feel a warmth and welcome and will be more inclined to return because of this individualized touch from their peers. Each teen in the youth group may have as many as four or five visitors under his wing that he is contacting each week and discipling after their conversion.

Activities

A fourth step would be to piggy-back activities with the youth leader of a large fundamentalist youth group across town or in a nearby town. Most good youth leaders would be glad to have another group join them on their big monthly activities, trips, or parties. Another approach would be to get four or five small churches (within a radius of twenty-five miles) of like faith and practice and plan joint activities. This cooperative effort enables a small group of teens to enjoy big activities and gives your teens the excitement and fellowship of a large group. A banquet, a skating party, or an Olympic day are held not just for the fun and fellowship but also for an evangelistic purpose. Unsaved teens will come out for a big party or activity with lots of teens, fun, and food, making it an ideal time to present the gospel.

Music

A fifth step is to get a good music program going with the teens. The leader may get a trio or quartet together that can give special numbers in the evangelistic meetings. The youth leader can get those who play instruments or sing solos to be part of the meetings. A small teen choir may even be started that can sing in the church service on some Sunday evenings. A good teen music program can appeal to a large segment of teens, especially girls.

Sports

A sixth step is to develop a Saturday morning competitive sports program within the group to attract teen contacts. Volleyball is ideal, for it can be played without expensive equipment or a large number of teens. Softball teams would be the next, then six-man touch football teams, and finally basketball teams if the use of a gym can be arranged. As the youth group grows, the number of teams in the program needs to be expanded. The visitors should be permitted to play on the teams even if they are not converted, for this program is being used to get them under the sound of the gospel. Every teen that comes out gets to play, and having fun is the key. The youth leader should limit the players to teen-agers but include both girls and boys. They must register so that they may be followed up as contacts for the group. Doughnuts, pop, and a gospel message in the middle of the morning enhance the program.

The sports program should be kept intramural, within the youth group, for when other churches and groups enter the picture, the leader must field a good team to win and must start weeding teens out. Ball games are then no longer a gospel recruitment tool, and the evangelistic purpose of the sports program is defeated.

A good sports program of this sort will draw the teenage boys. Just about every young man wants to be active in sports, but many do not feel that they are good enough to try out for a regular team. The Saturday morning sports program can give these young men an outlet.

Other Considerations

The youth group should be limited to high school teens and aimed at attracting young men. The temptation in a small church is to combine the high school group with the junior high and even with the juniors to increase the number. When such a large age group is included, the upperclassmen will drop out because junior highers are too immature and have different interests. And if the program appeals only to girls, it gives the impression that Christianity is just for ladies and children. But if the youth leader gears the majority of his activities to senior high young men, the girls will always come out to be where they are.

Friendliness is the key, making every visitor feel that he is someone special. The youth leader should attend the school games, plays, graduations, and other public school events, to make contacts and build the bridge of friendliness. One sports-oriented youth leader was made announcer at all the home games. The youth leader's high visibility at teen activities, fast-food eating places, and other spots where youth congregate helps them to feel that he cares and is interested in them.

A youth group can grow dramatically within a two-year time span if these six steps are followed. In fact, such growth happened in a six-month period in a church in Michigan, where the group increased from eighteen to over one hundred. As the adult church members see the growth and see teens coming down the aisle, they will be motivated to gospel action. Reaching new teens opens the witnessing door to parents, because they appreciate the positive changes in their children.

Once the youth group begins to grow, the teens may become somewhat fanatical in their gospel zeal. Their desire to have three consecutive all-night prayer meetings or to rent a plane to bomb the community with a million tracts should not be squelched. Instead, these ideas and energies should be rechanneled into productive outlets. A balanced, stable, enthusiastic youth leader following a proven plan can build a great youth group.

---

[1] See *Daws* by Betty Skinner, as referred to in Chapter 3.

Chapter 14
Parents and Lay Staff: Easing the Load

The successful youth leader will not overlook two important groups of people who can give the most assistance in building youth: parents and a lay youth staff. These adults are the often untapped resources in the youth ministry.

Parents

Parents are the youth leader's best allies in training teens for God's service. If the youth pastor is aware of some basic principles in dealing with parents, then his ministry will be strengthened and enhanced.

Recognizing ownership

The most important principle is that the teens belong to their parents and are their parents' responsibility. The church and the youth leader are helping the parents to perform their God-ordained role of building a unified home in which to train their children for God (Deuteronomy 6:1-4). The youth leader must continually strengthen the hand of the father and help him to build a strong home (Malachi 4:6; Ephesians 6:4). He can accomplish this job of helping the parents in several ways.

First, he can provide good books for them to buy and read. (Suggested titles are listed in Chapter 6). Some churches buy books on the family *(Formula for Family Unity),* on discipline *(Growing Up God's Way),* and on loving teens *(How to Really Love Your Teenager)* and give a copy to every family in the church.

Second, the youth leader can encourage the parents to go to family seminars and couples retreats. If scheduling or finances do not permit this, then he can rent a video seminar or an audio cassette series of messages on the home.

Third, he can encourage the parents to vacation at family camps where each member can make spiritual progress as well as have fun. Taking missionary vacations, during which the family helps a church or works at a mission station for two weeks, turns travel and sightseeing into blessing.

Fourth, the youth leader can hold parents' meetings once a month, perhaps on Sunday nights during youth time or Wednesday nights during part of prayer meeting. These meetings can be informative, letting the parents know about schedules, programs, and standards. Or they can be discussion and sharing times about problems or about desires the parents have for their teens. During the meetings, the leader can address typical parental concerns, such as television and video watching, curfew hours for different ages, the age at which teens should start dating, part-time and summer jobs, and peer pressure. The meetings can also be training times, giving the parents a synopsis of what the leader is teaching the teens, how to have family devotions, how to love teens, and how to prevent the generation gap through communication. (Surveys to get information for these meetings are given in Appendices G and H-2).

Fifth, the youth leader can suggest specific activities that fathers can use to promote unity in the family, such as having family night once a week, completing various family projects, taking adventure or historical trips, making special ways to celebrate holidays, and establishing family traditions. A list of suggestions for family unity (See Appendix F) can be given to the parents.

The youth director must alert the parents and teens to the enemies that have invaded the home and can eventually destroy it. He must recognize that the devil has easy access to the child in the average Christian home through built-in negative factors that appeal to the flesh and the "devil-dazzle" of the world (Ephesians 2:2-3). Some of these factors which the youth leader can help the parents to reduce or eliminate are as follows.

Father's neglect of and absence from the home   In the average church, only one out of ten Christian families has devotions or spiritual training in the home. It took a Supreme Court decision in 1963 to remove Bible reading and prayer from the public schools, but simple negligence on the part of a father takes it out of the home. The father's absence from the home beyond his regular work hours is also a negative influence. His other interests—including church work—keep him out of the house during most of the child's waking hours. Various studies show that the father's absence from the home causes boys in particular to be immature, peer-pressured, and more given to impulses than boys whose fathers are interested and involved in their sons' activities. Youth leaders can encourage fathers to give time and attention to their children and to family activities.

Mother's working full-time outside the home   Because of the materialistic emphasis of many Americans, families cannot balance a budget on one salary. The mother, then, is required to work full-time. In 1950 only 15 per cent of the mothers of school-age children worked outside the home. By 1985, not only had that percentage quadrupled to 62 per cent but also 49.5 per cent of the mothers of preschoolers and infants were brought into the work force. For the sake of the teen-agers-to-be, the youth leader should encourage mothers of young children to remain at home if at all possible to train and supervise their children.

Television viewing   In 1950 children watched on the average 20 hours per week of television. In 1985 they were watching 25.5 hours per week. Although the increase in quantity of time over those thirty-five years has been moderate, the decrease in quality of programming has been appalling, because sex, violence, rock music, and occultism dominate the content. The family roles portrayed are often incongruent with Scripture. This constant daily input cannot help corrupting children's minds. A good rule for families might be to pray and read the Bible as much as they watch television. The results would revolutionize Christian families.

Listening to rock music   Rock music has become the background of most television programs, including the commercials. According to rock musicians, the music itself is sexual and corrupting. Allan Bloom in *The Closing of the American Mind* states: "Rock music has one appeal only, a barbaric appeal, to sexual desire—not love, not eros, but sexual desire undeveloped and untutored. . . . Young people know that rock has the beat of sexual intercourse. That is why Ravel's Bolero is the one piece of classical music that is commonly known and liked by them."

Rock musicians stay on the leading edge of shock in order to sell more records. In the late fifties the words emphasized rebellion against authority, resulting in the rebellious sixties. In the sixties the emphasis was on promiscuity and drugs, ushering in a wave of these sins ten years later. The hits of the seventies promoted sexual perversions, including incest, masturbation, homosexuality, and bestiality; it is no wonder that the eighties heralded the onslaught of AIDS. In the eighties the words stressed occultism and suicide. So disturbing was this trend that the music industry was pressured into printing the words on the album jackets so that parents could censor what their children were listening to.[1]

Other negative factors that have an adverse effect on the home are bitterness of the parents or teens, inconsistent discipline techniques, and hypocritical Christianity.

Strengthening relationships

Another principle is that parent-teen relationships are strengthened by parent-teen activities. The youth leader can plan for father-son and mother-daughter banquets, competitive games with the parents and their teens on the same team, and afterglow meetings in the homes.

Maintaining contact

A third principle is that the youth leader must keep close contact with the parents. He can keep them up to date on schedules and activities by a monthly newsletter and a yearly calendar. The youth leader should also have informal visits with them wherever they are—in the barn, the garden, the shop, or the yard. He should be there in times of tragedy or emergency such as an auto wreck, surgery, a heart attack, or death in the family. He should be ready to give assistance or advice in times of family problems, such as a teen's running away, incest, separation, divorce, suicide, drunkenness, adultery, one of the parents' ending up in jail, or the father's losing his job.

Building respect

A fourth principle is that teens need help to respect and appreciate their parents' maturity, wisdom, and sacrifice. In their meetings the teens should get training on the authority, contentment, and servant principles and how to carry out these principles practically in the home. Once a year teens can host a parent-appreciation banquet, the highlight of which could be reading the teens' love and appreciation letters to their parents.

Most teens are to some degree impractical and idealistic, dependent while crying for independence, insecure, financially unstable, feeling oriented, and fairly sophisticated in sin. Parents, however, may feel that only their child has these problems. A youth leader's sharing his perspective on the normal teen-ager and teaching the information from Chapters 4 and 5 in parents' meetings can be a great boost to distraught fathers and mothers.

Supporting the family

Another important principle is that the youth leader must respect the holiday times, meal times, relaxing times, and bedtimes of the family. He should not take the teens out

173

on big activities, retreats, or missionary trips during Thanksgiving, Christmas, New Year's Day, or Easter. These are family unity times, and the youth leader should not disrupt them. The days between Christmas and New Year's, however, are a choice time to hold these activities.

Most families use the evening meal (around 6:00 P.M.) as perhaps the one time during the day when the whole family is together; therefore, the leader should not start meetings before 7:00 P.M. or hold an afternoon activity after 5:00 P.M., unless he is serving supper as part of the activity. Most parents are in bed by 11:30 P.M. or 12:00 midnight, and it takes a teen about an hour to get ready for bed; therefore, the youth leader makes sure that all the teens are home from regular meetings and activities by 10:30 P.M. so that the parents are not awakened by doors slamming, showers splashing, and drawers banging.

The youth leader can also arrange to have teen car pools with qualified teen drivers so that the parents do not have to interrupt their evening to make several trips. He might want to use a church bus to transport teens from certain parts of town.

Supporting the pastor

The final principle in dealing with parents is that the youth leader must be careful never to undermine the pastor. Disgruntled parents will be quick to pick up any differences of opinion between the youth leader and pastor. If the youth leader is not careful, some parents will try to use him as a way to attack the pastor. There are certain steps that the leader can take to keep from being used to undermine the pastoral authority.

He should meet with the pastor once a week to go over plans, activities, problems, and the total calendar. The leader should give a copy of the agenda to the pastor and get his agreement on everything that he plans to do. In this way the two leaders present a united front to the teens and to the parents. If the youth director and the pastor cannot agree on philosophy, the youth leader should quietly resign.

The youth leader is the eyes and ears of the pastor. Since the youth leader has such close contact with the families, and since teens are so open about family matters, he can be instrumental in helping the pastor to nip problems in the bud.

The youth leader takes dissident parents directly to the pastor rather than becoming their voice box. The youth leader must not be gullible and get in the middle of any pettiness and juvenile nit-picking. Many an idealistic, fresh-out-of-college youth pastor has been used by divisive church members to split a church and further their attempts to oust a veteran pastor.

The youth leader, through his programs, activities, teaching, and personal contact, can be of tremendous help to parents in their God-ordained role of training their children.

Lay Staff

As the youth group begins to grow beyond about forty teens, the church often realizes that it is becoming too big for the youth leader and his wife to handle by themselves. Where can they get help?

The answer lies in training a core of dedicated adults to serve as the lay youth staff. The youth leader should pray and look for a husband-and-wife team who is willing to be trained to work with youth. For every twenty teens added to the group, one couple should be added to preserve the ideal adult-teen ratio of one to ten.

Each couple must already have certain essential qualities. The best place to start is with a couple whose home life is right. Many of the teens come from unhappy or broken homes; they must have good models to show them what a good Christian home and family unity are all about. It is best not to use couples who have been divorced. The couple can be any age, but they must have the energy to keep up with teens. They must also be mature individuals who have the wisdom and discernment to moderate the wild excesses of youth without putting a damper on fun. They should be spiritual people who have regular personal devotions and memorize Scripture. A servant's attitude, with respect for authority and a loving, caring spirit, must be the outgrowth of their spiritual life.

After settling on these essentials, the youth leader looks for the following desirable assets in various members of his lay staff:

1. Fun-loving couples with a positive attitude add a flavor and excitement to the group.
2. Rugged outdoor types who are eager for challenges and adaptable to difficult situations are indispensable on long trips, hikes to the top of the mountain, retreats, and emergency times when some have to sleep on the bus or out-of-doors in sleeping bags.
3. A creative couple can be a big help with planning programs and decorations.
4. Mechanical or technical ability can be an asset in keeping the bus or the public address system running.
5. Athletic ability will enliven the sports competition.
6. Musical ability, especially in piano, will enhance the singing and boost the morale.
7. Some couples have the right qualities but no special assets and will make good "gofers," handymen, cooks, and bus drivers. They will relieve a lot of the load that wears out and distracts a youth leader from his main purpose.

The couples that the leader chooses should pray about the matter and then make a commitment to serve until God leads them out of the youth ministry. The average youth leader stays with a youth group only two years, so well-trained lay couples working with the youth help maintain a stable youth ministry during these times of transition.

Occasionally the lay workers should be asked to give their testimonies, lead in devotions, or speak if they have the ability. Through these opportunities, many a lay couple working with youth has been infected with the gospel challenge and ended up in the ministry or on the mission field.

The youth leader should have training and planning sessions with all his adult workers at least once a month, using this book and others, to make sure everyone has the same philosophy and approach.

The youth leader must learn to delegate jobs to these adult workers. One couple could be always responsible for the food, another for the room setup and public address system, another for the transportation and accommodations, and another for the program and music. Each couple should have a written job description that includes all of their responsibilities. The lay couples must in turn get the youth involved in doing all of these chores, for that is part of the teens' leadership training, and it keeps the couples constantly in contact with the youth group members. It is every couple's goal to get to know each teen in their care on a personal basis. If a couple has a teen in the youth group, that teen should be assigned to another couple.

The lay couples must recognize that the youth leader is in authority over them. The youth leader in turn must recognize the authority over him by checking all plans and exceptions to policy with the pastor when he meets with him weekly.

The youth leader will develop a team spirit among the staff by giving public praise and private reprimand. He should also keep the staff fully informed about any plans and any last-minute changes. He should meet with them once a year on a weekend retreat of some sort, preferably in December or August, to plan the next year's program, activities, trips, and schedules. This retreat is also an ideal time to give additional training by inviting a successful youth pastor to share his expertise and burden.

By developing the right youth staff and getting the full cooperation of the parents, the youth leader should be able to handle any size youth group.

---

[1] See "How Shock Rock Harms Our Kids," *Reader's Digest,* July 1988, p. 101.

Chapter 15

The Youth Leader's Wife: Contentment without Confusion

The wife of a good youth leader faces some distinct challenges, especially if she has two preschoolers and a baby on the way. Certain areas of her life must be rearranged to keep things from becoming complete chaos in the home and to avoid the spirit of bitterness and frustration that can easily develop. Her relationships to herself, to her husband, to her children, and then to the teens—especially the teen girls—are areas that need constant attention.

Herself

To overcome the feelings of inadequacy that plague most pastors' wives, the youth leader's wife needs to realize that God, in calling her husband, has also called her into the ministry. She is her husband's helpmeet and companion and is therefore part of the team. God will give her the same grace and power that He gives her husband. To fill her role properly, she will give attention to some definite personal goals for daily and weekly direction. She will list her goals, number them in order of importance, and then work to achieve them. Meeting goals will give her a sweet sense of accomplishment (Proverbs 13:12, 19).

In working toward goals, the wife needs to strike a balance between getting things done and dealing with people. Teens will show up at the house at all hours of the day or night. Though they may need help, she must put some limitations on her time with them in order to maintain family unity. The hours before 8:00 A.M. and after 9:00 P.M. should be private family times. Other private times might be family night, Sunday afternoon and evening, and supper time (between 5:30 and 7:00). Even taking the phone off the hook at these times may be necessary.

When teens drop by and she has much to do, she can let them help run errands or do certain chores. If teens need to discuss a problem, it is good for them to talk informally while they are helping with the dishes, cooking, doing housework, or taking care of a child. The wife needs to be prepared with some sewing, knitting, or other handwork so that she may sit and talk without feeling that she is getting behind in her work. Her goals must be flexible, for a great many problems in her husband's normal duties will alter mealtime, bedtime, recreational time, and even special occasions like their anniversary. She should not let these interruptions destroy her happy times or peace of mind; instead, she should be ready to reschedule, change plans, and adjust to the inevitable. Having several teen-age girls or other people on call to babysit in an emergency relieves some pressure. Having a relative or a sympathetic neighbor nearby helps tremendously.

One common problem can be jealousy. The youth leader's wife may feel threatened by the pretty, talented, and vivacious girls inevitably in the youth group who, she might think, are catching her husband's eye. If she is building up his ego, meeting his physical needs, adoring him and having daily times of fellowship and togetherness with him, she need not worry. He chose her as his wife because she was just right for him. She must help keep that flame of love ablaze by watching her weight and appearance and by keeping her eagerness and vitality, getting sufficient rest and exercise.

Another help is a sixth sense of propriety and intuition to warn her husband of "devil setups." These are situations such as the sweet little girl who wants the youth pastor to counsel her when her folks are not at home, or the lovely young lady who always wants to ride in the front seat when he is driving and insists on being taken home last so she can talk to him about a "spiritual problem." Girls will sometimes offer to babysit or to work in the home for free so that they can be near the youth director and be taken home by him late at night. The husband and the wife must agree upon certain ground rules for each other so that these situations will not arise. Here are some suggestions.

1. The youth leader will not be alone in a house or car with a female other than a family member.
2. The youth leader will not flirt, by kidding (which is part of the adolescent love line), touching, or being overly solicitous or complimentary.
3. The youth leader will never make suggestive remarks or thoughtlessly use terms of endearment with females other than his family members.
4. The youth leader's wife will do all the counseling of young ladies.
5. The youth leader and his wife will accept favors and attentions from young ladies as if intended for them both. (The wife will write the thank-you note to the girl for the cake intended only for the youth leader but enjoyed by both the leader and his wife.)
6. The youth leader and his wife will apply the principles found in I Thessalonians 5:22, Romans 13:14, and Romans 14:16.

Teen-age girls, especially junior high girls, tend to get crushes (intense emotional love feelings) on older, unattainable men. Though these intense, emotional love feelings are not serious, crushes can lead to real problems if not handled properly. The youth leader must be friendly but objective. Young ladies should never be ridiculed for their gushing, calf-eyed expressions of attention and love. The husband's response might be "Mary, I'm glad you enjoy the youth group and that my wife and I are such a blessing to you. By the way, were you and Jill able to finish the radio script?" If the girl states what an attractive husband the wife has, her response might be, "I think so too, and I hope one day you will have such a nice husband."

The youth leader should never be alone with this teen for extended periods of time, especially in counseling. Rather, he should arrange times when the wife or a female youth worker can do the counseling. Whenever the young lady comes around, the youth leader or his wife should always have something for her to do, to rechannel her desperate love feelings into work. Crushes are transitory emotions that will eventually dissipate if they are not encouraged.

The wife should not let the teen girls' sophistication shake her self-confidence. Teens feel very insecure, and this air of confidence and brashness is a cover-up. Underneath they have rejection problems and feel socially inadequate. The wife must be accepting and open to the girls with a heart of love. She speaks to every one of them with a smile, calling each by her first name.

Her Husband

The wife's relationship with her husband is crucial to the success of his ministry and the success of their children. The sweet unity that she maintains in her home will be reflected in her relationship with him in public. Teens like to see the tender touches, her willing submission, and his protective care for her as he assists her by opening doors and making her comfortable.

The wife must be careful about family discussions in public, for the teens easily misinterpret these as arguments and dissension. Neither the husband nor the wife should engage in the subtle art of put-downs, which can so easily occur in public and can be devastating to their testimony and even to their marriage. Teens are not the only ones who are offended by seeing one partner making the spouse the butt of jokes, interrupting the spouse to finish the story or to correct some unimportant point, making comparisons that put the spouse in an unfavorable light, using words or phrases such as "shut up" or "stupid," or making public the spouse's past or present bad habits and weaknesses.

The wife should support her husband one hundred per cent in his decisions and methods of doing things and should give any suggestions to him in private. She can be his right-hand helper by running the errand, handling the details, and covering his mistakes or forgetfulness. By knowing her husband's schedule and being able to reach him at any time, proofreading his printed materials, and accurately relaying telephone calls, the thoughtful wife helps her spouse to be efficient and on top of things. She should organize and plan schedules carefully so that she is always on time and never makes him late.

When others in the church criticize her husband without any justification, it is very hard for a wife to keep a sweet Christian response, especially if the chief critics are parents of the teens who have been given the most help. She has to prepare herself for this criticism, for it almost always comes to every youth leader. She must realize that it is impossible to please all the people all the time. Some parents object to teens' having fun because they never had fun in their teen years. Others are jealous of her husband's influence and his skill in communicating with the teens, especially if the parents are having problems with their own children. The people Satan sometimes uses to destroy a ministry are usually negative in all areas of life. The wife must let her husband handle the situation and must pray that God will give him the wisdom to help the critic. Above all, she must not let a root of bitterness spring up to defile her and her family (Hebrews 12:15 and Ephesians 4:30-32).

Her Children

If God has given children to the youth pastor's family, their training is a high priority. Children who lack training, attention, affection, and love in the preschool years have many problems later that can drastically complicate family life. The youth leader's wife will need to schedule enough time every day for her children—including fun times, story time, devotion time, character-building time, investigation time with lots of questions, Dad time, family time, and other times to be together.[1]

Joshua involved his whole family in his ministry when he said, "As for me *and my house,* we will serve the Lord" (24:15). The youth leader's children can be part of the ministry when they help work on the decorations, fix the hamburgers, serve, clean up, and enjoy the attention and excitement of being in the midst of a dynamic youth program. Teens will usually enjoy the children. One youth leader and his wife bought a camping trailer so their children could go with them on all the retreats, trips, and camps. On the other hand, if a mother is greatly involved in the ministry and leaves her children frequently with others, the children eventually view this separation as rejection.

As the leader's children get into grade school, they will be aware of various problems that occur in the youth group. These problems should be made a matter of family prayer, not to be discussed elsewhere, and the children will see how God solves the problems to His glory. But above all, the youth leader should not let a critical, negative, discontented spirit reign in the home (I Timothy 6:6). A complaining spirit (about the pastor, the salary, the living conditions, parents and church members) will do more to turn children away from Christianity than will anything else.

The Teen-age Girls

The wife's relationship with teens, and especially the girls, is crucial to her husband's ministry. She must get involved in the activities in which they participate, such as volleyball, tetherball, Ping-Pong, hiking, and skiing. If the girls are getting muddy in the tug-of-war mud pit, she should be right there pulling with them. Sleeping with them overnight in a tent at the bottom of Grand Canyon may be roughing it for a thirty-year-old mother, but it will help her to establish excellent rapport with the girls and to influence their attitudes.

She should try to get all the girls involved in games, and if a girl is standing on the sidelines, she could have the girl take her place on the team. By having the girls help in planning for, buying, and preparing food, putting up decorations, and performing other chores for the youth activities, the wife has a part in training the girls in practical service for the Lord.

Most youth leaders' wives feel it is essential to teach the teen-age girls' Sunday school class or have a Bible study class with them. Doing so helps them to keep up with the typical teen girl's problems and maintains a weekly close contact with all the girls. The weekly preparation also helps the wife to study the Word continually.

As the wife deals with girls in the youth group, she will find that many of the girls tend to be catty, talking about other teens in a negative manner. She cannot get involved in their petty squabbles or family arguments, nor can she play the role of a matchmaker or try to fix up their love life. She can give them general principles and guidelines but must not get bogged down in the blow-by-blow, day-to-day details. She can find other ways of being involved with the girls, such as taking them shopping, to the library, and on the many errands she has to run. Without showing partiality or playing favorites, the youth leader's wife stays ready to listen to the ones that are having problems or just need to talk. Having three or four girls over at a time for pizza or popcorn also gives the wife a good opportunity to sound them out.

For example, one wife was asked questions by four fifteen-year-old girls about French kissing and petting that had been going on. Their questions revealed a naiveté on the part of the girls and also a lack of dating standards among the youth in this church. This information prompted a series of messages on dating, as well as several parents' meetings discussing standards for the best age to allow a teen to start dating, types of dates, places to date, and conduct on dates. Also in separate sessions there was a series of messages on the purity principle (I Thessalonians 4:1-7) and the strange woman (Proverbs 5-7). The youth director's wife and a nurse talked very frankly to the girls, and a Christian doctor in the church joined with the youth director in talking with the boys.

As the wife counsels the girls, she must try not to condemn or be judgmental but rather to help them to apply the Bible principles that fit the problem or situation. She will counsel girls about vital problems such as incest, rape, pregnancy, drugs, running away from home, depression, and even severe mental problems, for these difficulties can be found in most youth groups. Other problems such as worldliness, smoking, movies, rock music, necking and petting, rebellion against parents, and lying are common occurrences. It will be helpful for the youth leader's wife to read several good books on counseling (suggested in Chapter 11) and then discuss with or refer to her husband or the pastor the difficult cases. She can identify the beginning of serious problems such as anorexia nervosa (a severe weight loss through controlled diet) and alert the parents to seek a doctor's help for their daughter.

She can give help and encouragement to the girls in other potential problem areas, such as dress, personal grooming, family relationships, dating standards, acne, posture, and weight control.[2]

In the husband's regular messages to the teens, he can handle many of the problems and give much information. The wife's awareness of the current problems and needs of the girls will enable her to feed this information to her husband so that his messages will meet the needs of the girls as well as the boys.

The youth leader's wife should constantly be helping the girls to apply the principle of respect for authority in their homes and giving them ideas on how to make contributions to family unity. (See also Appendix F.)

1. Expressing appreciation for the things that Mother does
2. Giving her regular compliments on her person, personality, and performance
3. Helping Mother and Dad to have time alone each week by babysitting the younger children
4. Taking responsibility for some of the household chores

5. Working alongside Mother while she cooks, serves, and entertains

Many girls do not get along with their mothers and attempt to drive a wedge between Mother and Dad. About ten per cent of the girls love their fathers more than they do their mothers and are jealous of their mothers. This unwholesome attitude can be a basis of teen-age incest in some cases, especially if the attitude has persisted for a long period of time. It would be the duty of the youth leader's wife to report this attitude problem to her husband so that he can take appropriate corrective measures.

Balancing her attention to the four areas of her ministry—herself, her husband, her children, and the teen-age girls—will help the youth leader's wife to have success and to enjoy her position thoroughly. If she is filled with the Holy Spirit and maintains an intimate relationship with Jesus Christ, eternal results are sure to follow her labors. And with a positive attitude of faith and praise, she will have the joy of the Lord as her strength (Nehemiah 8:10).

---

[1] For ideas for training children, see chapters 10-15 of *Formula for Family Unity.*

[2] Good sources for information in these areas are *FAMILY LIVING for Christian Schools* and *Beauty and the Best,* both published by Bob Jones University Press.

Chapter 16
Standards:
Aiming for Balance

Every youth leader must be concerned with the standards that he is going to set for his youth group. Youth are looking for standards because they are in the process of forming their own. To be effective, the leader's standards must be in general agreement with those of the pastor and the church in which he is working. He should not accept a position in a church with whose standards he cannot agree.

Perhaps the most important thing a youth leader can do in his ministry is to make practical application of truth. This is what Paul meant in Romans 12:1-2 when he urged the believers to give their bodies "a living sacrifice," and to "be not conformed" but rather "transformed." Heart and life transformations are the goal of Biblical standards and the evidence of applying God's Word to everyday life and behavior.

Kinds

In approaching the teaching of standards, the leader needs to keep several things in mind. First, there is, and always will be, a difference between institutional standards and individual standards. What may be necessary in an institution or organization to control hundreds or thousands of individuals may not be necessary for the individual himself.

The short haircut that a man wore in the marines may not be necessary for his normal functioning as a civilian after he retires. For youth activities, the leader will have to set some sort of standards—definite and clear rules of conduct for people to follow as they represent the church to the lost in their community. The individual, however, needs to be taught general and specific Biblical principles on which he can base his daily decisions and conduct, stressing obedience to Christ in every aspect of his life. The purpose of anyone who works with young people should not be to make standards for them but rather to teach them to make standards for themselves from God's Word.

Various youth programs not only have this very purpose but also provide the printed materials to help accomplish the purpose. For example, Pro-Teens (produced by Positive Action for Christ, Rocky Mount, N.C.) offers clear and practical materials designed to bring young people in Christ to maturity rather than rubber-stamping them with *do*s and *don't*s. The idea is to teach them how to make choices based on the Bible, not to make those choices for them.

Remember that institutional standards cannot be forced on individual lives and characters. It is the individual who fights temptation, who witnesses, who lives a testimony before neighbors. It is the individual who will give an account before his Lord Jesus Christ. Therefore, it is the individual who must search God's Word and set the standards of conduct that will govern his or her behavior for years to come.

A pastor, defending the "high" standards of a particular Christian college, once asked his congregation whether they really thought that God's standards were lower than the college's. One young man replied, "Maybe God's standards are neither higher nor lower, just different." The young man was correct in distinguishing rules of control from principles of daily living. Failure to recognize this difference will produce temporarily conformed teens rather than permanently transformed teens.

The Proper Attitude

The second important thing to remember is that heart attitude is the key to success in teaching standards. If there is a right attitude, the right standard will generally follow, with proper teaching. Teens should be fully informed about the Bible principles involved in an issue, and they should fully understand the battle with the devil that they are waging and the necessity of waging that battle according to those principles. The leader must get them fighting and thinking with him, not against him, by asking them to search out the Bible answers to issues, and by having them explain to their peers just what God has to say and how His principles apply. Young people naturally question most of what they are taught, so the youth leader should get them thinking along Biblical lines. He should teach them to ask, "But what does God say about this?" and then guide them in finding the Biblical answers.

It might be wise to remember the story of Solomon's son Rehoboam, related in II Chronicles 10. Instead of working with his subjects and getting them on his side, King Rehoboam "laid down the law" and provoked a rebellion that split the Hebrew kingdom. If the leader attacks his teens, he will provoke an attitude of defensiveness and rebellion. If he challenges them to think, question, and then decide to do what pleases God, he will for the most part win an attitude of cooperation and teachability.

The Purpose

The third and most vital thing to keep in mind is the ultimate purpose of any standard for the Christian: to help one toward the goal of personal holiness, not personal pleasure (I Peter 1:15-16 and Romans 12:1). That goal is best expressed in the command to "love the Lord thy God with all thy heart and with all thy soul and with all thy mind and with all thy strength" (Mark 12:30; Matthew 22:37; Deuteronomy 6:5).

Obstructions

Obstructing this goal are two warring camps of thought vying for the young Christian's attention: legalism and libertarianism. Either of them can sidetrack and spoil a sincere believer, distracting him from attaining the goal of personal holiness.

Legalism

Legalism in standards is a problem of focusing on the letter of the law, not the spirit. It is an attitude of mistrust rather than love, communicating from the leader to the youth group a total lack of confidence in them as disciples of Christ. It originates from one of two sources: a fleshly weakness in the faith or spiritual pride. The former is disruptive to a youth group, and the latter is destructive.

For the Christian who is saved out of a wicked background, legalism can be the result of a spiritual pendulum swing, a safety device to keep all the formerly loved temptations at a safe distance. Romans 14:1-2 and I Corinthians 8:9 describe the legalist as one who is weak in the faith. For this Christian, legalism is a defense mechanism, a reaction to a very real fear of his own weakness in the face of Satan's onslaughts. He has the right motives but the wrong focus. Rather than scorn a teen (or another youth pastor) for a legalistic attitude, the youth leader should remember Romans 15:1-2 and concentrate on bringing that person to an active, offense-oriented service for Christ instead of the reactive and miserable defensive response of legalism.

When the word "legalist" is mentioned, one automatically thinks of the Pharisees of Christ's day, and well he should, because the Pharisees epitomized the small-minded concern for the letter of the law over the spirit of the law. Their legalism, however, was not an innocent response to some fear of not pleasing God, but rather, as Christ pointed out in Matthew 11:17-19, it was a desire to control the lives and spiritual condition of others. The Pharisees wanted to make everybody dance to their tune, and obedience to them and their traditions was the only way to please them. Consistency is not a hallmark of this type of legalist; control and criticism most definitely are.

If the leader wants to see rebellion and bitterness take hold in his young people, he should control their lives, suspect their motives, and denigrate their spiritual desires with a harsh, legalistic attitude. Some men rule their flocks in this way, and it is these men onto whom the secular media latches. It is these men who give rise to groups such as Fundamentalists Anonymous. The password for an effective youth leader is love; the password for a legalist is power. Teens respond to love; they react to power.

Libertarianism

For the young Christian who comes out of a highly structured background of Christian education, or for the one who is accustomed to the oppressive atmosphere of legalism, the Biblical concept of liberty becomes a heady potion, and too many young people go overboard with their newfound spiritual freedom when this concept is first brought to their attention. There is no question that liberty is taught in the New Testament (in I Corinthians 8 and 10, Galatians, and Romans 14), but the danger lies in letting liberty become license.

There is a growing tendency among Christians everywhere to rationalize sin. If a particular verse has four interpretations, most Christians will choose the one interpretation that allows the most sin. When liberty is combined with self-will, licentiousness is the result. Therefore teens must understand both their liberty in Christ and the need to temper that liberty with love. As with legalism, love is the cure for this extreme view of standards.

When approaching the teaching of standards, the youth leader should not ignore or pass lightly over Christian liberty. He needs to teach it thoroughly and to encase the concept in the superstructure of love for a holy God and love for the brethren. As he points out to the teens that liberty should not be abused, he must explain that it should be governed by the following checks and balances.

1. God's direct commands (I John 2:3)
2. Edification of the brethren and themselves (I Corinthians 10:23, 33; Romans 14:7, 19 and 15:2)
3. Conscience (Romans 14:5, 6, 23)
4. Christ's reputation and their own (Romans 14:16)

By his own example and teaching, the leader needs to remind the teens that the object of standards is to help them toward the ultimate goal of personal holiness. Becoming like Christ, pleasing God and not self, is the goal. Setting personal standards is a means to that goal. Legalism and libertarianism are but rabbit trails on the path to holiness.

Strategy

What standards should the youth leader teach, and how should they be taught? The Bible clearly sets forth several overall principles, and from these principles specific applications can be made to specific situations. However, it is vitally important that each application also be Bible based. The most common problem confronting the youth worker who strives to teach standards is focusing attention on personal preference or some commonly held tradition rather than on God's Word and God's purposes. If the standard is not based on Scripture, then the youth group should not be conned into accepting it as a necessary step to holiness; for the result will be a cynical attitude in the young people. The youth leader should not let the standards be reactionary but rather make them active and purposeful.

Basing standards solely on Scripture immediately brings about several desirable results. First, it eliminates the establishment of myriad petty rules and regulations for the young people to have to follow; and second, it delineates a clear choice of obedience or disobedience in regard to the standards that ultimately are set forth. It also eliminates arguments over regionalism ("Where I'm from everybody does it") and background ("But my parents don't see anything wrong with it"). And it ultimately focuses attention on the heart attitudes of the young people, which is the key to their living victoriously.

Most teen-agers do not have to be convinced that certain things are wrong. Rather they need help in overcoming their addiction to these sin habits (Romans 6).

Areas

The following areas of concern, along with pertinent passages of Scripture, represent several of the most important general principles. However, this is not by any means meant to be considered a complete list.

Appearance

Dress standards can be guided by at least three passages: I Timothy 2:9, which emphasizes modesty, not drawing attention to the body; I John 2:15-17, which tells one where not to look for a source to imitate; and II Timothy 2:22, which, when taken in conjunction with Romans 14:13, cautions the young person about how his dress may affect another believer. The goal in setting dress standards is to avoid that which offends morally. It is important to note here that although the issue of appropriateness has validity in some instances (deep-sea diving outfits would not do for Sunday services), it never overrides the modesty principle. First Corinthians 11:3-16 sets forth general guidelines about hair length on men and women, but since these are very general, the emphasis should be on the heart attitude.

Morality

Standards of purity should be grounded in II Timothy 2:22 and I Thessalonians 4:1-7. Second Timothy 2:22 is the subject of much heated debate, but some unity can be attained by focusing attention on the first word, "flee," and defining it clearly as "run from," and then substituting "mother grizzly bear with cubs" for "youthful lust." It is amazing how much clarity and insight this little exercise provides as dating standards are discussed. This verse also provides a positive, active approach to dating standards, as the young people are taught to "follow after righteousness, faith, love and peace" and "a pure heart" when they are on a date. Second Corinthians 6 teaches whom not to date and why.

Entertainment and association

Standards of entertainment and association are guided by the principles set forth in Psalms 101 and 11:5. These principles eliminate virtually all network television programming, most movies, and most of the popular music. In the area of entertainment the stiffest resistance will probably be met, but again the emphasis is on holiness, not on what pleases the individual. A right heart attitude in the young people will result in an obedient response to the principles in these passages.

Music, especially Christian rock, will likely cause intense disagreement, and it is an area only vaguely dealt with in Scripture. However, Exodus 32:17-19 indicates that clamorous music with a noticeable beat accompanied the orgiastic, pagan worship of the golden calf. It was mistaken for war from a distance. Psalms 33:3 and 40:3 indicate a difference between the old, worldly and the new, godly songs. Ephesians 5:19 and Colossians 3:16 emphasize the importance of the Psalms, the old and respected hymns, and the melody (as opposed to harmony and beat). Christians have a tendency to do with music what the institutional Catholic church did with statues and holidays; we take our idols ("but I like it") and Christianize them. The result is not that the idol is made more holy but rather that Christian practices slowly become more pagan.

Physical care

Care of God's temple is covered in general by I Corinthians 3:16-17. This passage provides a starting point for teaching on gluttony, substance abuse, and harmful habits. The youth leader has to keep in mind that God and the youth group expect him to be the example in these areas. When a body-abuser preaches on this passage, audience receptivity understandably dwindles.

Focus

In all likelihood, every youth worker has something in his teen-age years of which he may not be especially proud. But it is important that a forgiven failure in the past should in no way hamstring the clear presentation of Biblical standards, even when the standard condemns past failures for all to see. The leader does not confess his past to the youth or base his teaching of standards on what he or someone else did or said, but on what God sets forth in His Word. He instills in young people a restless desire to know and honor God, to say not "I have a right to," but rather, "How can I bring honor and glory to Jesus Christ?" Then the teens will set high standards for themselves out of a desire to please God and not self, and they will do so when no one else is there to hold their hands.

Chapter 17
Activism:
Putting Principles into Practice

When speaking in parables to his disciples about the future of the world and Christianity in Luke 19, Jesus gave a command which, if obeyed by all Christians, could once again "turn the world upside down." He told them, "Occupy till I come." In the first years of the Second World War, as the German forces swept over Poland, Hungary, Czechoslovakia, Norway, and most of Western Europe, they left behind in each country enough manpower and equipment to maintain German domination. As evidenced by the drastic changes in the social, cultural, political, and religious fabric of the conquered nations, the military use of the word *occupy* means "to control or rule."

When Jesus told His disciples to "occupy," He decidedly did not mean to conquer and control by murderous force. But He also definitely did not mean that Christians were merely to take up space. Although sin has been with us since Adam, and the most vile practices known today have all been known before, never since the time of Christ has sin had such outspoken and shameless advocates, nor has Satan had such powerful mass media tools with which to spread so many lies in such a short time. The reason God's people are left on the earth after salvation is to perpetuate His kingdom by proclaiming the gospel and to battle the rapid advancement of Satan's kingdom. And that is what occupation is all about: actively controlling an area for the coming ruler—in other words, Christian activism.

Motivating

How can a youth leader lead his young people to war against Satan? First, he must lay the Biblical groundwork. By showing them the teaching of Christ on salt in Luke 14:34-35 and explaining the role of salt in purification and preservation, he can challenge the teens not to let the salt lose its savor.

He can also point out to the young people the Old Testament examples of what can happen when one or more dedicated people speak out and stand up for righteousness. Second Kings 23 tells of the sweeping changes made by one very young king, Josiah, who determined to wipe out all visible manifestations of sin among the people of his nation. In I Kings 18 the prophet Elijah publicly challenged the religious lies of his day, and God brought about a change in the hearts of the Israelites.

The young people need to see what Christ did in the temple (John 2:13-16), driving out the moneychangers. They need to read what He called the scribes and Pharisees (Matthew 23) and to be reminded that He said, "the servant is not greater than his lord. If they have persecuted me, they will also persecute you" (John 15:20).

Educating

After preparing the young people with the commands and challenges of the Lord Jesus Christ, stressing the forceful and bold manner in which Jesus and His disciples gave out the truth, the youth leader should draw the battle lines and educate the teens in the issues. He should show them how far Satan has advanced in society today and inform them of the ways in which Satan makes those advances. As the issues are dealt with, teens need to be directed to God's Word and to have spelled out for them in great detail what stand the Word requires them to take.

Although this education process should not consume all the leader's teaching and preaching time, it can be conducted very effectively by weekly reminders, updates, or notices. Five minutes a week taken to alert the teens of battles in which they personally can fight will keep them honed and ready for service, without making the subject seem trite and commonplace. As the youth leader does the educating, he should keep in mind that doctrine and spiritual growth should never be lost in a whirlwind of noble, feverish activity. He must keep in mind also that Christianity is a conquering faith, and that constant learning without faithful doing leads to stagnation and spiritual deadness (James 2:17).

There are innumerable organizations whose ministry is to keep Christians informed and involved, but some of the most effective are these: Focus on the Family radio and literature ministries with Dr. James Dobson; American Family Association with the Rev. Donald Wildmon; and the National Right to Life Movement, which has affiliate organizations in most states. There are several legal organizations that fight for morality or freedom of religion (including Citizens for Decency Through Law and the Christian Law Association) and organizations that publish materials to keep people informed of the battle lines being drawn in the courts and legislatures. Not every one of these groups would make a good source for ecclesiastical fellowship, but they all provide information, and information is what makes for intelligent decisions and actions.

Implementing

One thing that made the Nazi occupying forces effective was their seeming omnipresence. They struck fear into the hearts of the occupied peoples by making their presence known. If Christians do not likewise make their presence known, they are not obeying the command to occupy. The last step of Christian activism for the youth group is action.

They must act on the known information in a Biblical way. The objective for disseminating information is not to terrify young people into a state of paranoia or despair but to challenge them with the need for somebody to do something. The somebody should be the young people and the something, their actions. Teens can actively occupy for the Lord in three ways: winning souls, challenging lies, and protesting evil.

Winning souls

The action of primary concern is soulwinning, because changed hearts produce changed minds and lives, and such genuine change thwarts Satan's advances. Witnessing is doing battle on the front lines, where the resistance from the enemy is hottest; teens are understandably afraid to wage war in this area. The way to help teens overcome a fear of witnessing is to get them talking about Jesus Christ constantly, and the youth leader must lead the way. The leader must not show embarrassment, shame, or discomfort in speaking openly and lovingly about Jesus the Lord. And if the Lord is real to the youth leader, He will be real to the young people. They will see that He is not one to be ashamed of, but rather someone about whom they should talk more than they talk about sports, dates, or last night's television shows.

Soulwinning is facilitated by showing the unsaved the love of Christ through attitudes and reactions, community service, and loving deeds. The youth leader can find out who needs help and take the teens to help them. He can find out who needs food and have the teens gather and deliver it. When teens start looking around for ways that they can personally show the love of Christ, they often find permanent witnessing opportunities. Few experiences beat seeing firsthand what it means to earn the right to be heard.

Challenging lies

In the media, on television, in schools, and in the streets, Satan's lies about sin, God, creation, and righteousness are capturing the hearts of millions of unthinking or evil-thinking people in general and teens in particular. A good leader never lets a lie go unchallenged. This challenging of falsehood is "where the rubber hits the road" for the Christian teen, because persecution is very likely to result.

The right attitude is the key factor in responding to persecution. It has been said that an accusation provokes anger and defensiveness, whereas a question provokes thought. Therefore, teens should get into the habit of challenging lies with questions. For example, if a science teacher espouses evolution as an accepted fact in the public school classroom, the Christian teen need not jump up and scream "Liar!" Instead, he can make a simple request for a detailed and thoroughly logical classroom presentation of the "facts" of evolution from its beginning to the present, along with all the hows and whys. If the teacher accepts this challenge, the teen should calmly question every illogical step of the presentation. Christians must constantly question, turning the light of truth on the darkness of Satan's lies. If the attitude behind the questions is not one of arrogance or contempt, the unsaved classmates of the teen will be able to see the lie for a lie, and they will know that at least one person, the Christian teen, has an answer to the origins of life.

When pro-abortion, pro-euthanasia, or quality-of-life lies are heard in the classroom, on the job or anywhere else, a question sure to shock people into thinking is "Didn't the Nazis use those arguments to justify the gassing and shooting of the Jews, the mentally handicapped, and homosexuals?" While a question of that nature will certainly cause a commotion, it is better by far than calling everyone in the room a Nazi pig. Questions can be to the point, probing, and challenging. But the point is that the questions should be raised. As soon as the opportunity arrives for the Christian to present the truth, *The Bible says* should be the introduction to every statement. Without the Biblical groundwork previously mentioned, the teen-ager has nothing to present.

Protesting evil

When Satan's lies produce evil actions, the next step for the Christian teen is to protest evil. The weapons at hand in this battle are the pen, the telephone, and the sign. A church youth group can hold letter-writing sessions when the city or state legislature is voting on issues important to Bible believers. They can have phone parties to call government offices with polite protests of ungodly decrees or regulations. Teens can organize a march to protest abortion and carry their own hand-painted signs. Another effective approach is for all the teens in the youth group to tell the manager of their corner store that they personally do not appreciate his selling of pornography; or just as important, they should express appreciation for his refusing to sell pornography.

A strong leader will teach his youth group that a Christian should speak his mind, provided that the mind is filled with God's Word and is backed by a heart filled with God's love. He will let them see and experience the truth that God will work through His people if His people will just get to work. Activism is not an idea borrowed from the sixties' protest movements or the seventies' gay-rights scene. It is a principle of changing society through making a point of view known, and, for the Christian, activism means obeying Jesus Christ when He said, "Occupy till I come."

Internalizing

If there is to be a genuine difference, young people must be taught the qualities that will give them the resources to counteract the evil influences in their culture and to make some significant changes as they reach adulthood.

If a youth leader had the opportunity to see Jesus Christ on earth and to ask Him the reasons for the poor spiritual state of young people, what would His answer be? He would most certainly reply that those who train youth have not been giving the right emphasis and have not been teaching the qualities that would ensure spiritual growth and a change of the culture in God's direction. The emphasis in most youth groups and homes has been on sports, entertainment, comfortable facilities, academics, and a higher standard of living rather than on the spiritual training that the churches and homes were designed to give. The main qualities should be those He taught for three and a half years and that are taught throughout His Word in both the Old and New Testaments. A search of the Gospels and the whole Bible reveals these four dominant themes throughout: (1) faith, (2) love, (3) holiness, and (4) evangelism.

Faith

Bible faith starts at salvation. Faith cannot be properly developed until a person has a true born-again experience, getting his sins washed by the blood of Christ (Ephesians 1:7; John 1:12). This faith theme, developed in Hebrews 11, always involves hope, not only the hope of that eternal city (Hebrews 11:9-10, 16; 13:14) but also the blessed hope of the glorious appearing of Jesus Christ (Titus 2:13). Faith also involves a thorough knowledge of the principles of the Word of God. Romans 10:17 says, "Faith cometh by hearing, and hearing by the Word of God." Teaching your students to have regular devotions, to memorize Scripture, and to study thoroughly the Bible is very important in developing their faith (Psalm 119).

Trusting God when the circumstances are very bleak and seem to be working against them is also part of developing and strengthening their faith (Romans 8:28; Ephesians 5:20; I Thessalonians 5:18). (Most Christians have faith in God only as a last resort after their own efforts have failed.) Prayer and praise are essential in helping them to increase their faith (John 16:24; Psalm 107:8). As they see their prayers answered, their faith is strengthened. They begin to get a positive faith attitude (Philippians 4:8) instead of a negative devil attitude (II Corintians 10:5).

Love

Love is an unselfish, self-sacrificing desire to meet the needs of the cherished one. It involves understanding what the needs of the cherished person are, and then it involves giving to meet those needs (II Corinthians 9:6-8). God mentions in Matthew 22:37-40 that the two greatest commandments are to love God with all the heart, soul, and mind and to "love thy neighbour as thyself." First John 3-4 emphasizes that love is important and that God is love. A person who does not have love in his heart for people is not even born again.

An aspect of love is compassion that reaches out to relieve, to restore, and to cause to rejoice (Philippians 2:1-4). First Corinthians 13 gives the characteristics of love, and John 13:34-35 gives us a new commandment that we are to love others as ourselves. James 2:1-9 indicates that the royal law of love should not be violated by prejudice against poor people or any other kinds of people. Having a genuine love for Jesus Christ makes it very easy for us to love people. Love also involves an attitude of servanthood (Ephesians 5:21). Love helps us to be established in holiness (I Thessalonians 3:12-13; Romans 13:8-14).

Holiness

Sin and the flesh have an influence but no controlling power over the born-again Christian (Romans 6:1-22). In the power of Christ, he can live a life of holiness. God demands holiness (I Peter 1:15-16). Without holiness no man shall see the Lord (Hebrews 12:14). The believer's body has become God's temple (I Corinthians 3:16; 6:19), and God wants him to keep His temple holy. Maintaining holiness requires self-discipline (Romans 13:14; 14:16; I Thessalonians 5:22) and a proper reaction to God's discipline (Hebrews 12:10-13).

Magnifying God's holiness always demands honesty (Ephesians 4:25; I Peter 2:12), purity (I Thessalonians 4:1-7; Ephesians 5:3; I Peter 2:11), and separation from the world (James 1:27 and 4:4; I John 2:15-16; and II Corinthians 6:14-17), and from ecclesiastical compromise (Galatians 1:8-9; II John 9-11).

Evangelism

The great commission was given in all the Gospels and Acts. First Corinthians 15:34 says, "Awake to righteousness, and sin not; for some have not the knowledge of God; I speak this to your shame." God could have broadcast the message from the sky every hour, but instead, He chose Christians to herald the message. Christians need to practice constantly the five steps of evangelism: (1) inviting people to church and gospel services; (2) carrying and passing out tracts; (3) giving personal witness—telling people how they were saved, using a number of Scripture verses on salvation so that the person can hear the Word of God, be convicted, and be saved (Romans 10:13); (4) winning a person to Jesus Christ and then discipling and teaching him all things (II Timothy 2:2); and (5) finding a ministry—a Sunday school class, bus route, jail service, child evangelism class, etc. Even children and teens can take these five steps and be trained in evangelism (Psalm 126:5-6).

The big question is how these four themes can best be taught to our young people so that they will internalize the qualities and have a good influence in their culture. With the right actions, each one can have an impact.

1. Daily emphasize and model these four qualities and make them lifelong standards to be constantly exhibited before others.
2. Teach and preach these qualities in Sunday school, in devotionals at activities, at camp, and in discussions with teens.
3. Check on the young people and help them to check on themselves as they implement these four qualities in their lives.
4. Initiate various projects which allow them to put these qualities into practice. For example, help the teens to decide to put love into practice by taking as a love project the eighty-year-old widow who lives down the street. They could prepare supper for her, clean her house, rake her leaves, dig the flower beds, and take her to the grocery store every week.
5. Pick out three born-again leaders in the youth group, pray for them daily, and teach them these qualities. Urge these leaders to live by these principles, constantly

measuring their lives by them and seeking daily guidance from God.

It is only through the power of Jesus Christ working in and through born-again Christians that anything can be accomplished. "Without me ye can do nothing" (John 15:5). Born-again teens must decide that they are going to influence the culture in which they live by living and teaching these qualities. When the teens reach adulthood, their children will be greatly affected as they observe their godly parents. In the community, neighbors will be affected as they see Christians manifesting these qualities. In business, corporate leaders will be influenced as they see their partners and employees living these qualities. There will be revivals in churches if Christians decide to make the changes to bring their lives into line with God's qualities. If any changes are going to come about in our culture in the next generation, they will be determined by what born-again Christians do with these qualities today.

Chapter 18
The Youth Group vs. the Christian School: Conflict or Cooperation?

If there is a Christian school in the church with a good, comprehensive program, is there a need for a youth ministry program? Doesn't the Christian school perform all the functions and have all the activities that the youth program would have at the church? If there is a need for a youth ministry, is it even possible for a good, aggressive youth program and a dynamic Christian school to exist in a church without one program overriding and destroying the other? Is there any way to avoid the competition between the Christian school and the youth program for the teen-agers' time, facilities, activities, and budget? What is the purpose of the Christian school and the youth ministry? Do they exist mainly for evangelism or for edification? These are legitimate questions facing churches that have both a Christian school and a youth ministry. Even the youth leader of a small church with no Christian school of its own may serve youth from one or more Christian schools; he too must consider these questions.

Understanding the Problem

Les Ollila, president of Northland Baptist Bible College, compiled a number of concerns voiced by youth directors during his ministry as a youth pastor and conference speaker.[1] One of the major ones is that the sports program is becoming the main purpose of many Christian schools. The teens are developing a greater loyalty to the school and the sports heroes than they are to Jesus Christ, the Bible, the church, and the pastoral staff. According to many youth directors, the sports program seems to be inculcating the wrong values and attitudes in the average Christian school teen-ager's life.

Wayne Haston[2] says that the number one difficulty is the competition between the two ministries trying to control the same activities. Number two is the obvious overlap in the teaching ministries of the youth group and of the Christian school. Number three is the conflict over control of the facilities such as the buildings, the meeting rooms, the equipment, and even the library. Number four involves the concern of parents that their teens are overly busy, because the Christian school and the youth activities absorb all the teens' free time and even the family time. Number five is the apathy in teen evangelism because of a loss of contact with unsaved teen-agers. He points out the tendency for the Christian school teens to form cliques and to cut the public school teen-agers out of youth group activities, consequently stifling teen evangelism.

In his article, Haston proposes a way to coordinate activities, programs, facilities, budgets, and the teen-agers' time by getting a master calendar and having the youth director and the principal work together to present a coordinated ministry to the youth. Then in staff conference, held at least once a week, the pastor would make all the final decisions about the function of the youth ministry and the function of the school.

This problem was again addressed in 1982 in a book by Paul Bubar entitled *The Jericho Wall.* In the typical church, Bubar believes, the Christian school swallows up the youth ministry. He suggests that the youth ministry be dedicated mainly to evangelism and the Christian school to the edification of the saints. He observes that as the youth activities become centered in the Christian school, the evangelization of the lost public school teens is completely eliminated from the church. This phenomenon occurs because the schools' natural mission is edification of Christian youth, not evangelism.

He finds that the average Christian school has several definite assets: a qualified staff, a philosophy, a curriculum, a chain of command, a budget, and communication with its workers and with the pastor. The typical youth ministry, by contrast, has either none of these qualities or very few of them. He issues a challenge to youth pastors to develop these six areas so that they will be as qualified to minister to youth as Christian school administrators are. Then he appeals to the school to take its proper position as an institution of education and edification, and for the youth group to take its proper position as an evangelistic arm of the local church ministry. He sees the youth ministry as a strong soulwinning, discipling, and recruiting ministry, aiding the Christian school and the local church. He emphasizes that if the youth ministry is swallowed up and the youth activities and sports programs are taken over by the Christian school, then the evangelistic thrust of the church to unsaved youth will die. Eventually the Christian school will be hurt, because new converts will not be fed into it.

Without question, this conflict does exist in most larger churches with thriving Christian schools; and it is usually the youth ministry that is sacrificed to the Christian school. As a Christian school takes over the church facilities that the young people use, as it puts on all the activities that the youth attend, and as the total school program and curriculum encompass all that the youth are to learn, there is little time or reason left for the students to participate in any type of youth ministry. As the youth program begins to diminish, so does the evangelistic outreach to the unsaved teens in the community. The Christian school then tends to become a sterile, self-serving entity of the church and does not give the teen-agers a complete program of carrying out the Great Commission.

Defining Roles

The solution to the problem can be found in determining the purposes of the youth ministry and the Christian school. The church exists to carry out two main functions: (1) evangelism—soulwinning and discipling (Matthew 28:19-20; Mark 16:15; Luke 24:27); and (2) edification—teaching Christians how to worship God and to do the work of the ministry as they are conformed to the image of Christ (Ephesians 4:12-13; Romans 8:29). But which function is better carried out by the youth ministry and which by the Christian school?

The youth group

The main function of the youth ministry might better be evangelizing, discipling, and building the character of the youth in the community. The various activities of the youth group would then be designed to reach the unsaved and help the Christian teen-ager carry out the evangelization of his peers. The focus of the youth meetings would primarily be to build character, to disciple, and to train youth to become full-time servants of Christ.

A secondary purpose of the youth ministry would be to provide activities, programs, and experiences that cannot be carried out in the home. Because the home lacks the number of teens and the facilities required for certain activities such as team sports, film presentations, and banquets, a good youth group is necessary. These activities and experiences should help the youth put into action the Bible principles they are learning in the home, the church, and the school. However, good youth groups will not minimize or crowd out the functions of the home; rather, they will supplement and strengthen the influence and importance of the home in the training of the teens.

A third purpose would be to provide a social environment where teens can have healthy social contacts with members of the same sex and of the opposite sex.

A fourth purpose would be to offer teens and their parents a counseling service that provides Bible answers for the personal and family problems that occur in most people's lives.

A fifth purpose would be to help teens grow through Bible study and memorization, and then to encourage them to use this knowledge to reach out to others through discipleship programs. The youth ministry should become the avenue for teens putting into practice the evangelistic principles they have learned at home, at church, and in school. It is a proving ground on which they come to grips with the claims of Christ in changing peoples' lives.

The Christian school

The main function of the Christian school, on the other hand, might better be edification: helping to conform the individual to the image of Jesus Christ (Romans 8:29). The home has been given the mandate to train, educate, and edify (Ephesians 6:4; Deuteronomy 6:11-12); and much of the edification must be done at home in family Bible studies, devotions, discussions, and individual counseling. However, the average Christian home today does not have the facilities or qualified personnel to teach the academic fundamentals and the large variety of subjects that the student needs to learn in order to live successfully in our complex society. Therefore, Christian schools have been established to assist the parents in giving a Christian viewpoint and a Bible basis for every subject. The school should be the place of academic learning; teachers in the school help the students to make practical applications of that learning.

The specific purposes of a Christian school could then be stated in the following way.

1. To give the basic tools of learning so that the students might read, write, and compute with comprehension.
2. To provide a reservoir of Bible doctrines and Bible principles that students can use to analyze, evaluate, and judge the learning that they receive in every subject.

3. To provide a background in various subject areas (including terms, definitions, general principles, ideas, and related Bible principles) so that students will have a storehouse of information from which to draw as they interact with the world and face the practical problems of life.

4. To give a foundation in specialized subjects for future vocational development in the students' chosen field of service.

5. To develop a sensitivity to beauty and an appreciation of culture, especially the godly heritage and the beautiful things of life that God has provided for them.

Keeping these purposes in mind, teachers should bring practical experiences right into the classroom through good filmstrips, cassette tapes, and videocassettes. A school should also teach practical subjects such as typing, home economics, computers, and mechanical or architectural drawing. These subjects would not necessarily be major areas but perhaps form the nucleus of a practical vocational program for those students who are not interested in further academic pursuits.

In the senior high school a good course on the family ought to be taught. The course should include lessons about developing a Biblical self-concept, decision making, efficiency, mature conduct, dating relationships, engagements, weddings, and basic Bible principles of having family unity and happiness in marriage. Students also need information on parenthood, training children, financial responsibilities, and how to have leadership and good management in the home.

Restructuring Organization

The main purposes of the youth group—evangelism—and of the Christian school—edification—are not mutually exclusive domains. Evangelism is certainly one of the happy results in both groups. However, by its very nature the Christian school can more efficiently and effectively emphasize edification; for its function is mainly education based on Bible principles, and an unsaved young person does not receive or understand spiritual teaching (I Corinthians 2:14). Most Christian schools require a thorough initial interview with both the parents and the child and include a strong gospel presentation at that time. If the parents agree to cooperate with the school's Christian education of this child, entrance policies of the school can permit the enrollment of some unsaved students, especially on the elementary level. The elementary school should then maintain a strong evangelistic emphasis to win these young people to the Lord. On the high school level, because of the unsaved student's peer influence, wrong future goals, and behavior problems, a school is wise to limit the unsaved student's enrollment to one year if he does not respond to the gospel. In some situations, the same principle should apply on the junior high level. To prevent corruption of the whole school, it is imperative that the student leaders all be spiritual Christians.

The youth ministry, on the other hand, although it should certainly involve itself with edification, has as its main purpose evangelism. Both groups seek to help the youth be conformed to the image of Jesus Christ (Romans 8:29). By determining the unique purpose of each, a leader can begin to develop a coordinated program, enriching all the youth through both the youth ministry and the school.

Coordinated programs, rather than competing programs, come about as the youth leader and the school principal meet at least once a week with the pastor, working out a master program and calendar for the year. They should discuss the times at which the teens are going to be at various activities, the facilities that the groups are going to use, the subject matter of the curriculum, and the various types of activities that have been designed for the youth. Such weekly meetings would also coordinate the standards of conduct and the program of evangelism carried out by the youth.

The practical applications of this coordination are described below.

Schedules

Teens must have time for their families. They must have time for their work and for the activities that their parents want them to do. Therefore, the leaders must be careful that the youth group and the school do not take up a great deal of the teens' home time after school through evening activities and excessive homework. The youth group and school activities should be scheduled on only two or three evenings a week, leaving free evenings for family unity times.

Facilities

Generally facilities should be shared; however, certain facilities, such as the library, will be exclusively the school's, since most of the books are for educational purposes. As a service, the school could run the church library and the youth library on Sundays. The school also might want to administer the church bookstore, where books are sold to members at reasonable prices.

Naturally the school would use the gym for physical education classes and team sports during the school day and for any interscholastic sport practices and games after school. They would schedule the use of the gym or multipurpose room for any parent-teacher meetings, student registration, or other activities demanding a large facility. But a gym, especially one with a fireplace at one end or in one corner, could be the main meeting room for the youth group as well. An ideal gym would be much like a multipurpose room, with a kitchen at one end for holding banquets and fellowships, and a stage to one side for dramatic and musical activities put on by the school or the youth group.

Ideally, classrooms would be designed for the school but would have folding walls that could transform a large school classroom into smaller Sunday school classrooms. Many of the school classrooms could have acoustical folding walls between them so that the rooms would be versatile, transforming regular school classrooms into big rooms for larger church activities.

Curriculum

The school curriculum and the youth curriculum must be coordinated. Probably the school will try to include more intensive study of the Word of God, such as Bible doctrine, prophecy, dispensations, and church history. The youth ministry, then, would make the messages and lessons more topically oriented, teaching Bible principles about character development, dating, marriage, divorce, authority, keeping a clear conscience, forgiveness, and various other principles that build character.

Activities

The activities of the youth group and the school should be coordinated. The physical education classes of the school should focus on exercise and on teaching the basic skills of various sports that the students can use to keep their bodies in good physical shape. The teaching would concentrate on fundamental skills and rules of soccer, baseball, basketball, flag football, tennis, racquetball, bowling, and volleyball. The school should also emphasize physical fitness through activities such as jogging, weight lifting, and gymnastics. The local YMCA pool might be available for teaching lifesaving and other swimming skills. If there is a nearby lake, even canoeing and rowing can be taught there as a part of the physical education program.

While the school may have its interscholastic sports teams and competition, the youth group should run an *intramural* sports program, involving both the public school and the Christian school youth and involving every member of these groups. The youth group's sports program can be designed to attract unsaved youth so that the sports program can be used as a method of evangelism. The men's and women's teams of the church could all be coordinated through the youth pastor.

The youth group's monthly or weekly program would include all kinds of activities for fun and evangelism. (See Chapter 7.) These would all be designed with an evangelistic purpose—to gain an effective point of contact for presenting the gospel to young people. The gospel message would be a part of every monthly activity—not just a devotional but a regular gospel challenge with an invitation. For the Christian youth attending the youth activities, the main purpose would be to make their contact with the unsaved or with the new converts they are following up and discipling.

Standards

The standards of conduct, appearance, and dress must be the same for both the Christian school and the youth group. However, these standards cannot apply to the unsaved public school youth that are being attracted to the youth ministries' evangelistic efforts. The youth leader and the school principal must work together to establish standards that will neither turn away unsaved youth from activities nor make the Christian youth feel that there is a double standard in the church. The Christian teens must be aware of the difference that exists between them and the unsaved.

Achieving Balance

The youth group program can be designed primarily for carrying out the Great Commission: reaching others with the gospel, teaching them to observe all things, and making them into reproducing Christians according to II Timothy 2:2. The youth ministry provides the avenue for communicating to others the truths learned in school.

The main purpose of the Christian school can be educating and edifying the believers. A good youth group should feed new converts not only into the church but also into the Christian school so that they can be educated for full-time service for the Lord.

If this kind of program is to be implemented, it will require a well-trained, full-time youth leader with the same qualifications that the Christian school leadership has. He should have a sound Christian philosophy of education, be an aggressive, Spirit-filled soulwinner, have strong character, and be able to train young people in Bible principles. A full realization of the different purposes of the youth group and the Christian school will be the balancing factor between the two groups as they work together to train youth—training them to be conformed to the image of Christ and to glorify God with lives completely dedicated to His service.

---

[1] "Church/School Conflicts," *Pro-Maker,* September/October 1977, pp. 7-9.

[2] "Developing Harmonious Christian School and Youth Ministry Relationships," *Pro-Maker,* January/February 1980, pp. 13-15, 28.

Chapter 19
Compromise:
Bending to External Forces

As seen from the history of youth work in Chapter 3, it is very difficult for a non-church-related youth ministry to stay on the Biblical track. Even church-related youth groups can have the same problem. Virtually every youth leader faces the temptation to compromise—particularly in the areas of music, methods, manner of dress, and message—in order to reach more young people.

Recognizing the Pressures

Some of the pressures for this compromise are suggested below.

Unconventionalism

It is easy for creative youth workers to feel that conventional churches are too stilted and legalistic, putting barriers between dynamic, flesh-oriented, immature youth and the gospel. Since teens are given to extremes that shock the staid pillars of the church, some feel the only way to reach action-oriented youth is to get them out of the worship-oriented church into an organization where they can be themselves.

However, when a group gets away from the organized local church, it gets away from the steadying influence of older, mature Christians; the result is a pandering to youth's extremes and excesses in the four areas mentioned above.

Mass evangelism

With the youth leader's strong zeal for winning souls to Jesus Christ, he may have a tendency to use all kinds of methods without regard for Biblical principles or for the justifiable concerns of others. For example, suppose that his church sits on a hill, overlooking a valley and beach area where thousands of people congregate on the weekend. He decides that every Saturday and Sunday afternoon he is going to blast the area with good music and the straight, hard-hitting gospel message from his superspecial souped-up PA system mounted on the steeple of the church. Or he determines that the youth group will pass out tracts and hold a gospel service in the big shopping mall on Saturday, without the mall management's permission. Or he realizes that typical rock concerts are crowded with teen-agers; so he decides that his group will sponsor a gospel rock concert in the local high school auditorium so that all the teens in town can hear how to be saved both in song and in preaching.

When standards of decency, propriety, or appropriateness slip, the view of God's holiness begins to be clouded, and soon any method and means are used to win people to Christ.

Love for the brethren

Born-again believers experience a wonderful love and fellowship. They share their experience of salvation by grace through faith and rejoice in the cleansing of sin through the blood of Jesus Christ. Some may become disillusioned with the narrow provincialism and typical exclusive attitude of many Christians, and doctrinal differences on baptism, church affiliations, the type of music, and the mode of worship begin to seem very insignificant. From this dissatisfaction there arises a desire to cooperate with other believers in the great universal church fellowship. Finally the tendency is to become inclusive to the point of accepting anybody who professes belief in Jesus Christ in any way. When this kind of inclusive fellowship has been reached, Bible truth has been compromised.

Financial needs

As a youth group, a camp, or other youth gospel work begins to expand, it requires more money to operate—perhaps more than the fundamentalists are willing to give. In order to broaden their financial base, the administrators look to more liberal groups and even to those who are not committed Christians. This pressure is especially strong when the group has overextended itself financially. The leaders are tempted to do everything and anything to make the payments and keep the organization from foreclosing. At this point the Biblical principle that the borrower is servant to the lender comes into play. The leaders must serve the creditors instead of Christ; therefore, they water down the gospel message and eliminate any standard that would alienate other people, especially businessmen who might be interested in contributing. Churches with Christian schools or big building programs can put great pressure on the youth leader or school principal to relax standards or avoid disciplinary action that would upset the parents and affect the financial status. Compromise is an inevitable consequence of this policy.

Wolves in sheep's clothing

In every organization the devil makes sure that he has his agents to wreck and destroy. They often appear to be very good Christians who become board members, lay workers in the group, or even teen leaders. As the youth leader sits in committee meetings with these workers and hears their proposals, his tendency may be to make small compromises on principles just to keep peace and avoid offending a valuable member of the organization. Instead, he must take a stand against these wolves in sheep's clothing and be firm on principles. It might even come to the point of asking that person to resign or ousting him from the membership. Usually friends get offended and cause a stir among the brethren. But not taking strong action in the face of these pressures results in an organization that becomes compromising and corrupt.

Success

Many leaders like to feel that they are building a successful organization—numbers, outreach, and increasing budget are usually their measurements of success. When they begin to see a decline in these three areas, they tend to panic and to do everything possible to turn things around and get them moving ahead again. They start letting the end justify the means and make pragmatic decisions that affect the group's spirituality.

False tests of spirituality

The pressure of the works approach to holy living puts the youth group back under the law. Although a letter-of-the-law judgmental attitude may not appear to be compromise, it makes extra-Biblical rules a false test of spirituality. The book of Galatians reminds us that saints are under grace by faith, and it specifically warns against putting saints back under the works of the law and counting these works as righteousness or spirituality.

A blameless testimony is of great value, and a youth group might choose to abide by specific rules and regulations to operate efficiently and effectively. Rebellion against these rules and the authority behind them does indicate a spiritual problem. However, Christians must not judge other families and groups because they do not hold to those same extra-Biblical standards. The youth leader will be pressured, perhaps by well-meaning parents, to produce teens conformed to a particular standard; it is far easier to do this than to produce teens transformed into the image of Christ. However, the stifling works-of-the-law approach will produce pharisaic teens, and it eventually will stifle evangelism, fracture the youth group, and finally kill it.

Countering the Pressures

The best defense against pressures to compromise is operating on Bible principles in a spirit of love. If a youth leader continually declares, teaches, and operates by Bible principles, people start expecting him to act and react in certain predictable ways. Some may call the leader closed-minded, stubborn, inflexible, and ultrafundamentalist; but he will be known as having Christian character, a spirit of love, and a sound Biblical philosophy to which teens can relate. Teens react against mean-mouthed, vicious Christians who have bitter, prejudicial spirits; and intelligent teens have an idealistic sense of fairness. They get disturbed when Christian leaders violate the royal law of love (James 2:8; John 13:34-35; Matthew 22:36-40).

As the leader's philosophy is grounded in the Word of God and he is fully aware of the holiness of God as contrasted with the sinfulness of man, the institutional standards, regulations, methods, activities, and teaching will remain on the right course. His labors will be to the glory of God, and he will see eternal results.

Chapter 20
Qualities of the Successful Youth Leader:
The Icing on the Cake

The youth leader, whether salaried or volunteer, should consider himself as a youth pastor and therefore should have the same qualities that are necessary for a successful pastor. What qualities should he acquire that will turn his preparation into successful service for the Lord?

Success is knowing God's will and faithfully doing it. It is God's will that a youth leader or a pastor be filled with the Holy Spirit, have an intimate relationship with Christ, pray without ceasing, lead a holy life, get the gospel to the uttermost part of the earth, rule well his own household, preach the Word, and carry out the commandments of loving God with all his being and his neighbor as himself. Successful youth leaders and pastors who do those things also have the following qualities.

1. They have a burning desire to reach as many people as possible with the gospel of Jesus Christ, knowing that "faith cometh by hearing, and hearing by the Word of God" (Romans 10:17).They seize every opportunity to win souls, pass out tracts, disciple new converts, and support missionaries and other Christian workers. They have gotten on the gospel trail, and they believe it is always "too soon to quit." For instance, a seventy-five-year-old pastor retiring to Florida started two Bible clubs and was appointed as a staff visitor for a local church within two months of his arrival.

2. They have unconditional friendliness. They are "people persons" without prejudice. They have that open friendliness in approach, voice, stance, and gestures. They go out of their way to be friendly. This attitude, of course, creates many witnessing opportunities for them. One pastor who traveled frequently was known for his ability to win waiters and waitresses to the Lord because of his friendliness.

3. They have a servant's attitude. They have a heart of love for people and will do almost anything for anyone at any time. Yes, sometimes people take advantage of them, but they let God balance things out. They would rather give money than lend it, and they always have a bed and a meal for anyone in need, especially Christian workers and missionaries. A pastor of a large church in a large city used to drive along the highway with mechanic's tools and a five-gallon can of gasoline in his trunk. He would look for people stalled on the side of the freeway so he could help them and witness to them.

4. They are goal setters. They write down their daily, weekly, monthly, and yearly goals. They number them in order of importance and then pray about what God wants them to do, knowing that God will not load them down to the point of exhaustion or of hurting their fellowship with Him or their family. They are flexible under the leadership of the Holy Spirit so that God can work out His own plan and goals in their lives. A youth leader of a large rural church youth group has his goals—"visions of the future" as he calls them—set ten years ahead.

5. They always have a positive attitude of faith. Their approach is to praise the Lord and let Him run the show. Even when things seem to be going all wrong, they give thanks in every situation, knowing that God is in control and is working all things together for good. A certain youth leader of a large youth group has had chronic physical difficulties, a deformity, tragedy in his parents' home, and a sudden financial reversal; yet he has allowed the Lord to bring him through those trials and has maintained a rejoicing, positive faith testimony through it all.

6. They have an enthusiastic attitude. Anything they do, they do wholeheartedly (Colossians 3:23). Enthusiasm is based on good planning and on flexibility when the best-laid plans go awry. Enthusiasm can be genuine only when one knows what he is going to do and how he is going to do it. Uncertainty is the death of enthusiasm. Teens get enthusiastic when their leader is excited about the activity, project, or event. These youth leaders want to do everything to the glory of God, and they give one hundred per cent to even the most mundane things in their lives. One well-known youth leader used to make a big event out of eating a salad or cleaning up after an activity, and this enthusiasm carried over into everything the youth group did. An abundance of energy is helpful in maintaining an enthusiastic spirit. A "Praise the Lord" attitude is evidence of enthusiasm.

These six qualities are developed through an intimate relationship with Jesus Christ and a willingness to follow His commandments (John 14:21). Young men in the youth ministry who are cultivating these qualities cannot help being successful youth leaders for God.

Appendices

Appendix A
Bible Action Truths

Christian teens today need to be part of a truly Christian youth group. Our purpose, of course, is to train youth to have sound Christian character to do the Lord's work and to glorify His name. Therefore, our teens must learn to attain God's goals by applying Biblical principles; when their actions are consistently in line with Bible truths, they will have Christian character.

We do not train Christian leaders with character merely by teaching them 10,000 facts in six years. Character can improve only as youth leaders identify strengths and weaknesses and teach their teens to grasp fundamental Bible principles upon which to base their actions. Bible principles provide solid, absolute beliefs for daily actions.

Great Christian youth leaders know how to teach Bible truths in principle form and how to integrate all other material with this truth. Unfortunately, many Christian youth groups lack principled instruction based on the Bible's guidelines for action. Many students coming from Christian schools have been taught a lot of secular knowledge with Bible classes and chapel added; but they do not know basic Bible principles, and they do not know how to integrate knowledge with these principles. The thirty-seven Bible Action Truths listed here are suggested as foundations for principled teaching and are conveniently classified under eight action-reaction headings.

There are thousands of Bible truths; those listed are the ones most directly affecting character. These principles can be used as the foundation for Bible study in the youth group. They are also foundation stones upon which the entire youth group should be established.

A balance in using these principles is important. It is easy to overemphasize one or two Bible truths and neglect all others, causing warped and maladjusted reactions. There are many different ways of teaching these truths. The proper utilization of Bible Action Truths will enrich learning and lead the teen to a useful, balanced, and well-adjusted Christian life.

Of course, these principles are intended for the young person who has been born again and who is being taught the important doctrines of the Bible. Many Bible principles can be used by unsaved people, and they will work because their effectiveness depends on God's power and promise rather than man's condition. But an unregenerate man or woman is not inclined to follow Bible principles because he does not have the fear of the Lord (Proverbs 8:13) and because he does not really understand Bible truth (I Corinthians 2:14). Salvation brings the fear of the Lord, which is the beginning of wisdom and knowledge (Proverbs 1:7, 9:10).

A truly Christian youth leader points teens to the Bible, the absolute guide for living; he teaches them the principles in this guide and helps them learn how to implement these principles. Young people need to grasp Bible principles and make them part of their lives.

Real success in a youth group can be measured by the number of teens who are successfully serving the Lord and who are actively practicing Bible principles in their daily lives. Admittedly, the youth group cannot accomplish its task without the cooperation of the home. Both must work together to build character in the teens. The goal is a high one; but when home and church work together in a systematic way, that goal can be reached.

1. Salvation—Separation

Salvation results from God's direct action. Although man is unable to work for this "gift of God," the Christian's reaction to salvation should be to separate himself from the world unto God.

   a. Understanding Jesus Christ (Matthew 3:17; 16:16; I Corinthians 15:3-4; Philippians 2:9-11) Jesus is the Son of God. He was sent to earth to die on the cross for our sins. He was buried but rose from the dead after three days.

   b. Repentance and faith (Luke 13:3; Isaiah 55:7; Acts 5:30-31; Hebrews 11:6; Acts 16:31) If we believe that Jesus died for our sins, we can accept Him as our Saviour. We must be sorry for our sins, turn from them, confess them to God, and believe that He will forgive us.

   c. Separation from the world (John 17:6, 11, 14, 18; II Corinthians 6:14-18; I John 2:15-16; James 4:4; Romans 16:17-18; II John 10-11) After we are saved, we should live a different life. We should try to be like Christ and not live like those who are unsaved.

2. Sonship—Servant

Only by an act of God the Father could sinful man become a son of God. As a son of God, however, the Christian must realize that he has been "bought with a price"; he is now Christ's servant.

   a. Authority (Romans 13:1-7; I Peter 2:13-19; I Timothy 6:1-5; Hebrews 13:17; Matthew 22:21; I Thessalonians 5:12-13) We should respect, honor, and obey those in authority over us.

   b. Servanthood (Philippians 2:7-8; Ephesians 6:5-8) Just as Christ was a humble servant while He was on earth, we should also be humble and obedient.

   c. Faithfulness (I Corinthians 4:2; Matthew 25:23; Luke 9:62) We should do our work so that God and others can depend on us.

    d. Goal setting (Proverbs 13:12, 19; Philippians 3:13; Colossians 3:2; I Corinthians 9:24) To be faithful servants, we must set goals for our work. We should look forward to finishing a job and going on to something more.

    e. Work (Ephesians 4:28; II Thessalonians 3:10-12) God never honors a lazy servant. He wants us to be busy and dependable workers.

    f. Enthusiasm (Colossians 3:23; Romans 12:11) We should do *all* tasks with energy and with a happy, willing spirit.

3. Uniqueness—Unity

No one is a mere person; God has created each individual a unique being. But because God has an overall plan for His creation, each unique member must contribute to the unity of the entire body.

    a. Self-concept (Psalm 8:3-8; 139; II Corinthians 5:17; Ephesians 2:10; 4:1-3, 11-13; II Peter 1:10) We are special creatures in God's plan. He has given each of us special abilities to use in our lives for Him.

    b. Mind (Philippians 2:5; 4:8; II Corinthians 10:5; Proverbs 23:7; Luke 6:45; Proverbs 4:23; Romans 7:23, 25; Daniel 1:8; James 1:8) We should give our thoughts and minds to God. What we do and say really begins in our minds. We should try to think of ourselves humbly as Christ did when He lived on earth.

    c. Emotional control (Galatians 5:24; Proverbs 16:32; 25:28; II Timothy 1:7; Acts 20:24) With the help of God and the power of the Holy Spirit, we should have control over our feelings. We must be careful not to act out of anger.

    d. Body as a temple (I Corinthians 3:16-17; 6:19-20) We should remember that our bodies are the dwelling place of God's Holy Spirit. We should keep ourselves pure, honest, and dedicated to God's will.

    e. Unity of Christ and the church (John 17:21; Ephesians 2:19-22; 5:23-32; II Thessalonians 3:6, 14-15) Since we are saved, we are now part of God's family and should unite ourselves with others to worship and grow as Christians. Christ is the head of His church, which includes all believers. He wants us to work together as His church in carrying out His plans, but He forbids us to work in fellowship with disobedient brethren.

4. Holiness—Habit

Believers are declared holy as a result of Christ's finished action on the cross. Daily holiness of life, however, comes from forming godly habits. A Christian must consciously establish godly patterns of action; he must develop habits of holiness.

    a. Sowing and reaping (Galatians 6:7-8; Hosea 8:7; Matthew 6:1-8) We must remember that we will be rewarded according to the kind of work we have done. If we are faithful, we will be rewarded. If we are unfaithful, we will not be rewarded. We cannot fool God.

    b. Purity (I Thessalonians 4:1-7; I Peter 1:22) We should try to live lives that are free from sin. We should keep our minds, words, and deeds clean and pure.

c. Honesty (II Corinthians 8:21; Romans 12:17; Proverbs 16:8; Ephesians 4:25) We should not lie. We should be honest in every way. Even if we could gain more by being dishonest, we should still be honest. God sees all things.

d. Victory (I Corinthians 10:13; Romans 8:37; I John 5:4; John 16:33; I Corinthians 15:57-58) If we constantly try to be pure, honest, and Christ-like, with God's help we will be able to overcome temptations.

5. Love—Life

We love God because He first loved us. God's action of manifesting His love to us through His Son demonstrates the truth that love must be exercised. Since God acted in love toward us, believers must act likewise by showing godly love to others.

a. Love (I John 3:11, 16-18; 4:7-21; Ephesians 5:2; I Corinthians 13; John 15:17) God's love to us was the greatest love possible. We should, in turn, show our love for others by our words and actions.

b. Giving (II Corinthians 9:6-8; Proverbs 3:9-10; Luke 6:38) We should give cheerfully to God the first part of all we earn. We should also give to others unselfishly.

c. Evangelism and missions (Psalm 126:5-6; Matthew 28:18-20; Romans 1:16-17; II Corinthians 5:11-21) We should be busy telling others about the love of God and His plan of salvation. We should share in the work of foreign missionaries by our giving and prayers.

d. Communication (Ephesians 4:22-29; Colossians 4:6; James 3:2-13; Isaiah 50:4) We should have control of our tongues so that we will not say things displeasing to God. We should encourage others and be kind and helpful in what we say.

e. Friendliness (Proverbs 18:24; 17:17; Psalm 119:63) We should be friendly to others, and we should be loyal to those who love and serve God.

6. Communion—Consecration

Because sin separates man from God, any communion between man and God must be achieved by God's direct action of removing sin. Once communion is established, the believer's reaction should be to maintain a consciousness of this fellowship by living a consecrated life.

a. Bible study (I Peter 2:2-3; II Timothy 2:15; Psalm 119) To grow as Christians we must spend time with God daily by reading His Word.

b. Prayer (I Chronicles 16:11; I Thessalonians 5:17; John 15:7, 16; 16:24; Psalm 145:18; Romans 8:26-27) We should bring all our requests to God, trusting Him to answer them in His own way.

c. Spirit-filled (Ephesians 5:18-19; Galatians 5:16, 22-23; Romans 8:13-14; I John 1:7-9) We should let the Holy Spirit rule in our hearts and show us what to say and do. We should not say and do just what *we* want to do, for those things are often wrong and harmful to others.

d. Clear conscience (I Timothy 1:19; Acts 24:16) To be good Christians, we cannot have wrong acts or thoughts or words bothering our consciences. We must confess them to God and to those people against whom we have sinned. We cannot live lives close to God if we have guilty consciences.

e. Forgiveness (Ephesians 4:30-32; Luke 17:3-4; Colossians 3:13; Matthew 18:15-17; Mark 11:25-26) We must ask forgiveness of God when we have done wrong. Just as God forgives our sins freely, we should forgive others when they do wrong things to us.

7. Grace—Gratitude

Grace is unmerited favor. Man does not deserve God's grace. However, after God bestows His grace, believers should react with an overflow of gratitude.

a. Grace (I Corinthians 15:10; Ephesians 2:8-9) Without God's grace we would be sinners on our way to hell. He loved us when we did not deserve His love and provided for us a way to escape sin's punishment by the death of His Son on the cross.

b. Exaltation of Christ (Colossians 1:12-21; Ephesians 1:17-23; Philippians 2:9-11; Galatians 6:14; Hebrews 1:2-3; John 1:1-4, 14; 5:23) We should realize and remember at all times the power, holiness, majesty, and perfection of Christ, and we should give Him the praise and glory for everything that is accomplished through us.

c. Praise (Psalm 107:8; Hebrews 13:15; I Peter 2:9; Ephesians 1:6; I Chronicles 16:23-36; 29:11-13) Remembering God's great love and goodness toward us, we should continually praise His name.

d. Contentment (Philippians 4:11; I Timothy 6:6-8; Psalm 77:3; Proverbs 15:16; Hebrews 13:5) Money, houses, cars, and all things on earth will last only for a little while. God has given us just what He meant for us to have. We should be happy and content with what we have, knowing that God will provide for us all that we need. We should also be happy *wherever* God places us.

e. Humility (I Peter 5:5-6; Philippians 2:3-4) We should not be proud and boastful but should be willing to be quiet and in the background. Our reward will come from God on Judgment Day, and men's praise to us here on earth will not matter at all. Christ was humble when He lived on earth, and we should be like Him.

8. Power—Prevailing

Believers can prevail only as God gives the power. "I can do all things through Christ." God is the source of our power used in fighting the good fight of faith.

a. Faith in God's promises (II Peter 1:4; Philippians 4:6; Romans 4:16-21; I Thessalonians 5:18; Romans 8:28; I Peter 5:7; Hebrews 3:18—4:11) God always remains true to His promises. Believing that He will keep all the promises in His Word, we should be determined fighters for Him.

b. Faith in the power of the Word of God (Hebrews 4:12; Jeremiah 23:29; Psalm 119; I Peter 1:23-25) God's Word is powerful and endures forever. All other things will pass away, but God's Word shall never pass away because it is written to us from God, and God is eternal.

c. Fight (Ephesians 6:11-17; II Timothy 4:7-8; I Timothy 6:12; I Peter 5:8-9) God does not have any use for lazy or cowardly fighters. We must work and fight against sin, using the Word of God as our weapon against the Devil. What we do for God now will determine how much He will reward us in heaven.

d. Courage (I Chronicles 28:20; Joshua 1:9; Hebrews 13:6; Ephesians 3:11-12; Acts 4:13, 31) God has promised us that He will not forsake us; therefore, we should not be afraid to speak out against sin. We should remember that we are armed with God's strength.

The 4M Formula (from Psalm 119)

1. Mark these Bible Action Truths during your Scripture reading (verse 9).
2. Memorize the verses which best represent the truths (verse 11).
3. Meditate on the verses throughout the day (verse 15).
4. Master these Bible Action Truths in your daily life until they master you (verse 17).

Appendix B
Bible Quiz Teams

Rules

- A Bible Quiz Team consists of five players and up to four substitutes, from grades seven through twelve. The team must have a captain and a co-captain.
- A quiz consists of twenty questions, each worth twenty points, over a specified portion of Scripture. An incorrectly answered question incurs a ten-point penalty.
- A quizmaster is appointed to read the questions and to decide whether the answer given is satisfactory. He should have an assistant to watch the lights (in order to tell who jumps first) and keep the time, a statistician, and a scorekeeper.
- The quizmaster calls the quiz to order by saying, "Question."
- If a quizzer moves from his seat before the question is finished, he must both finish the question and answer it correctly.
- A period of five seconds from the time the quizmaster finishes the question is allotted for the quizzers to respond. Once a quizzer is recognized, he has five seconds to begin his answer, and fifteen seconds to finish it. If he fails to begin or finish his answer within the time allotted, he is considered to have answered the question incorrectly.
- In the event that a quizzer fails to finish a question correctly or give a correct answer, he is penalized ten points and the question rebounds to the corresponding member of the other team (each team's seats are numbered 1-5 from the quizmaster's left). The quizzer stands, the question is repeated in full, and he has the full allotted time to begin and finish his answer. If his answer is correct, it is worth twenty points; he is not penalized for an incorrect answer. The quizmaster then proceeds to the next question.
- A quizzer will be removed from the quiz in the event that
    1. He fouls out (answers five questions incorrectly).
    2. He quizzes out (answers five questions correctly).

    3. He is replaced with a substitute.
- Substitutions may be made when
    1. A quizzer fouls out.
    2. A quizzer quizzes out.
    3. A time-out is called. (The time-out must be called by a team captain or, in the event that he is not in the quiz, the co-captain, and it may not be called after the fifteenth question.)
- The quiz must end on a correctly answered question (not a rebound).
- The key to Bible quizzing is motivating the quizzers.

Strategy

I. How to study individually
    A. The quizzers
        1. Memorize their entire passage.
        2. Become able to associate a verse with its reference.
    B. The coach
        1. Knows and understands the material.
        2. Writes several questions on each verse for quizzers to study.
II. How to practice as a team
    A. Procedure
        1. Practice twice a week (Wednesday/Saturday or Wednesday/Sunday practices are best) with the coach as quizmaster.
        2. Set up the room like a quiz platform.
        3. Keep the practice quiz as authentic as possible.
            a. Follow ALL the rules.
            b. Word the questions as the quizmaster would word them.
            c. Provide incentive for the quizzers to give one hundred per cent during practices.
    B. Practice
        1. Never leave a question unanswered or not understood by each quizzer.
        2. Direct questions to specific people occasionally.
        3. Concentrate on the passages the young people know least.
        4. Practice jumping.
    C. As the coach, stress a positive faith attitude toward the competition.
III. How to choose starters
    A. Choose sometime during the week just prior to the meet.
    B. Choose the top performers in the practices to be the starters.
    C. Choose the top two performers to be the captain and the co-captain. The captain should, if possible, be a male, in order to stress male leadership. This is a good motivation point for the boys.
IV. How to conduct the quiz
    A. Carefully observe the progress of the quiz so that you can advise your team wisely.
    B. Make substitutions fair and practical.

     1. Use as many players as possible, especially when far ahead or hopelessly behind. (fairness)

     2. Do not substitute at crucial points during a match. (practicality)

C. Emphasize sportsmanship.

     1. Insist on a positive attitude and a good testimony regardless of what happens during a quiz.

     2. Teach the team members to congratulate a winning team or compliment a losing team.

D. Stress a positive faith attitude.

For electronic scoring equipment write to the following address:

     Quiz Teams
     P.O. Box 551
     Benton Harbor, MI 49022

For questions and a rule book write to the following address:

     GBC Christian Education
     P.O. Box 365
     Winona Lake, IN 46590

Appendix C
Recipes for Large Groups

BEEF BARBECUE
(50 servings)

12 lbs. beef roast	12 c. water
4 c. chopped onion	3 c. catsup
2 T. mustard	1 T. Worcestershire sauce
3 T. salt	¾ c. flour

Cook beef in a large covered pan, with some water added, on stove top for 2 hours. Mix together the rest of the ingredients except flour; at the end of 2 hours, add this mixture to the meat and cook 1 hour longer, or until meat is tender. Remove meat from pan; use a fork and break the meat into small pieces. Return to broth. Measure out 1 c. broth and stir in flour until mixture is smooth. Add to meat and stir well. Continue cooking until broth has thickened.

HAMBURGERS
(100 servings)

22-23 lbs. ground beef	6 c. milk (or 4 c. milk
$\frac{1}{3}$ c. salt	and 2 c. tomato juice)
4 t. pepper	6 c. bread crumbs (7 c. if
1½ c. minced onion	juice is used)

Mix all ingredients until well blended. Form into patties, using about one-third cup per patty. Fry quickly in a small amount of oil. To keep patties warm, put into a pan, cover with foil, and put into an oven at 200°.

MEAT LOAF
(100 servings)

20 lbs. ground beef
2 lbs. ground pork
2½ lbs. day-old bread
2 c. chopped onion
½ gal. whole milk

1 doz. eggs, beaten
$\frac{1}{3}$ c. salt
2 t. black pepper
2 c. catsup, tomato sauce,
   or tomato puree

Soak bread in some water; squeeze out excess moisture and discard water. Combine bread, meats, onion, milk, eggs, salt, and pepper. Mix well. Shape into loaves and place close together in greased baking pans. Bake at 325° for 1½ hours.

SLOPPY JOES, No. 1
(50 servings)

8 lbs. ground beef
1 c. chopped green
   peppers (2 medium)
6-8 medium onions,
   chopped
½-1 c. flour

1 T. salt (or to taste)
3 T. Worcestershire sauce
8 c. catsup
½ t. Tabasco sauce
2 T. celery seed
1 t. chili powder

Brown ground beef with peppers and onions. Stir in flour and salt until smooth. Add remaining ingredients and stir until well blended. Bring to a boil; turn heat low and simmer 20 to 30 minutes, stirring occasionally.

Note: If ground beef is exceptionally fat, spoon off the excess fat before serving. Two to three pounds more meat may be needed to allow for shrinkage.

SLOPPY JOES, No. 2
(150 servings)

25 lbs. ground beef
9 green peppers, chopped
20 medium onions,
   chopped
13 c. chopped celery
¼ c. salt

8 12-oz. cans tomato paste
5 tomato-paste cans water
2 c. vinegar
1 c. mustard
½ c. sugar
Worcestershire sauce to
   taste

Brown meat with peppers, onions, and celery. Drain off excess fat. Add remaining ingredients and bring to a boil. Turn heat low and simmer 45 minutes.

BAKED BEANS
(100 servings)

24 lbs. dried beans,
   navy, or No. 10 can, pinto
12 lbs. (or less) salt
   pork or bacon, cubed
3 lbs. onion, chopped
¾ c. salt

½ c. dry mustard
4 c. brown sugar
2 gal. or 2 No. 10 cans
   tomato sauce
2 c. molasses

Rinse beans. Cover with cold water and soak overnight. Drain. Add fresh water to cover beans and cook slowly (at simmering point) until beans are tender, about 1½ hours. Add water as needed, but *only* enough to come to top of the beans. Add remaining ingredients and pour into large pans. Bake at 300° for 4 hours. (If beans are done before baking, bake one hour.)

For a change, add 180 hot dogs cut into fourths.

FRENCH TOAST
(100 servings)

13 1-lb. loaves bread
4 doz. eggs

2 T. salt
1½ gal. milk

Beat eggs; add salt and milk. Heat skillet with margarine until hot. Dip bread into egg mixture. Brown bread on both sides until lightly browned. Keep warm in the oven at 200° until ready to serve.

ITALIAN SPAGHETTI
(100 servings)

18 lb. ground beef
4-6 green peppers,
   chopped
1½ c. dried onions
3 No. 10 cans tomatoes
2 T. salt
1 No. 10 can tomato
   paste

3 c. water
2 T. celery salt
2 T. onion salt
2 T. garlic salt
1½ c. sugar
40 lb. spaghetti
10 1-lb. cans Parmesan
   cheese

Brown ground beef with peppers and onions. Add remaining ingredients. Bring to a boil. Turn heat low and simmer 2-3 hours. Serve over spaghetti with Parmesan cheese.

Cook spaghetti according to directions on box.

MACARONI AND CHEESE
(100 servings)

6½ lbs. macaroni
4 lbs. medium cheddar
  cheese, grated
2 lbs. butter or margarine

4 c. flour
2 gals. milk
6 t. salt
4 t. paprika

Cook macaroni in boiling salted water (1 gal. water per pound of macaroni) about 20 minutes. Drain and rinse in cold water.

Melt butter over medium heat. Stir in flour until smooth. Add milk and salt. Cook, stirring constantly, until sauce is thick. Stir in cheese and paprika. Add macaroni to sauce. Pour into large pans. Bake at 350° for 20-25 minutes.

Note: You may use nonfat dry milk and reconstitute milk as directed.

PANCAKES
(100 servings)

9 lbs. (36 c.) flour
8 oz. (1⅓ c.) baking
  powder
4 T. salt
1½ lb. sugar

2 doz. eggs
6 qts. milk
1½ lb. (3 c.) margarine,
  melted

Sift together the first 4 ingredients. Combine eggs, milk, and margarine. Add to dry ingredients and mix thoroughly. Cook on greased griddle or skillet until each is full of bubbles. Turn to finish cooking. Put in oven at 200° to keep warm.

COLE SLAW
(100 servings)

16 lbs. finely chopped
  cabbage
2 qts. vinegar
⅔ c. salt
3 lbs. (9 cups) sugar

1 gal. mayonnaise or
  cooked salad dressing
1 No. 10 can crushed
  pineapple, drained

Mix all ingredients together well. Chill until ready to serve.

POTATO SALAD
(100 servings)

24 lb. potatoes, boiled
   and cubed (19 qts.)
4 qts. (4 lbs.) chopped
   celery
4 doz. boiled eggs,
   chopped

4 c. chopped onion
1 qt. sweet pickle relish
4 T. salt
1 c. vinegar
1 qt. mayonnaise or
   cooked salad dressing

Mix together the first 5 ingredients. Stir salt, vinegar, and mayonnaise together. Pour dressing over the potato mixture and stir well. Chill until ready to serve.

Note: The salad improves on standing; so prepare early. Also, it is better if mixed together while potatoes are still warm. Do not mix in tin, or potatoes will darken.

COCOA
(100 servings)

6 c. sugar
4½ c. cocoa
1 t. salt

1 qt. warm water
1½ gal. boiling water
3½ gal. hot milk

Mix together sugar, cocoa, and salt. Add warm water and mix until smooth. Add boiling water and boil 10 minutes. Add to hot milk.

APPLE CRISP
(50 servings)

10½ lbs. cooking apples
1½ c. sugar

Streusel

Peel, core, and slice apples in a bowl; stir in sugar. Arrange in a large greased pan. Cover with streusel. Bake at 350° for 50 minutes.

Streusel

1½ lbs. butter or
   margarine
6 c. flour

2 lbs. brown sugar

Mix flour and sugar together until well blended. Cut in butter until mixture forms fine crumbs.

CHOCOLATE CAKE
(100 servings)

4½ c. shortening, softened	4 T. soda
14 c. sugar	4 T. baking powder
5 c. cocoa	3 T. salt
29 eggs, beaten	11 c. milk
20 c. flour	1 T. vanilla

Cream shortening and sugar together until fluffy. Add cocoa and mix well. Add egg and beat thoroughly. Sift flour, soda, baking powder, and salt together; add alternately with milk, starting and ending with flour. Add vanilla. Bake in well-greased, well-floured pans at 375° for 25-30 minutes.

OATMEAL COOKIES
(100 cookies)

4 c. shortening, softened	5 t. vanilla
5 c. brown sugar	5 c. flour
2½ c. sugar	3 t. salt
5 eggs	2½ t. soda
1¼ c. water	3 c. oats

Cream together shortening and sugars. Add eggs, water, and vanilla and beat well. Sift together flour, salt, and soda; add dry ingredients to shortening mixture, mixing well. Stir in oats. Drop by teaspoons onto greased cookie sheets. Bake at 350° for 10-15 minutes.

Note: Chocolate chips and nuts may be added; ¼ t. cinnamon and ¼ t. nutmeg will make spice cookies.

Appendix D
First Aid
for Camps and Youth Activities

Basic First-Aid Kits

Hiking and athletic shed kits

1. Alcohol pads
2. Betadine pads
3. Sting-relief pads
4. Band-Aids
5. Telfa pads
6. Gauze pads
7. Kling
8. Compress
9. Tape
10. Triangular bandage
11. Ace bandage
12. Ice pack
13. Safety pins
14. Matches
15. Tweezers
16. Monojel
17. Salt tablets
18. Paper bag
19. Ammonia inhalants
20. Benadryl capsules
21. Epinephrine and syringe
    (Follow doctor's orders.)
22. Paper and pencils
23. Emergency codes

Lake kits

Same as above plus sterile needles for removal of splinters

Maintenance First-Aid Kits

Vehicle and shop kits

1. Alcohol pads
2. Betadine pads
3. Sting-relief pads
4. Band-Aids
5. Telfa pads
6. Gauze pads
7. Kling
8. Tape
9. Triangular bandage
10. Tweezers
11. Sterile needle
12. Ammonia inhalant
13. Benadryl capsules
14. Aspirin or Tylenol

Crew kits

1. Cleanup and special crews (same as vehicle kits)
2. Ground and painter crews (in small containers)
   a. Band-Aids (4)
   b. Betadine pads (4)
   c. Sting relief pads (4)
   d. 2″ × 2″ gauze pads (4)
   e. Ammonia inhalant (4)
   f. Sterile needles

Wilderness First-Aid Kits

Same as basic first-aid kits plus the following:

1. Aspirin
2. Lomotil
3. Tylenol
4. Triple antibiotic ointment
5. Rhulicream
6. Steristrips
7. Snakebite kit
8. Scissors

Medicase

1. Air splints
2. Cervical collars
3. Rib belts
4. Stethescope
5. Blood pressure cuffs

First-Aid Kit Contents

Dressing supplies

1. Betadine pads
2. Band-Aids
3. Telfa pads
4. Gauze pads
5. Kling
6. Compress
7. Tape

Orthopedic supplies

1. Triangular bandage
2. Safety pins
3. Ace bandage
4. Ice pack

Splinter supplies

1. Alcohol pads
2. Tweezers
3. Sterile needles (optional)

Hyperventilation supplies

1. Ammonia inhalant
2. Paper bag

Sting and allergic reaction supplies

1. Sting-relief pads
2. Benadryl capsules
3. Epinephrine and syringe (Follow doctor's orders.)

Miscellaneous supplies

1. Salt tablets
2. Monojel
3. Matches
4. Paper and pencil
5. Aspirin (optional)

Allergic Reactions

Mild local reaction

(Moderate swelling around the sting; NO respiratory distress)

1. Give Benadryl—1 or 2 capsules
2. Let victim rest—sit or lie down
3. Apply ice to sting

Severe systemic reactions

(Respiratory distress present, dizziness, etc.)

1. Inject 0.3 ml epinephrine into upper arm; may repeat in 20 minutes if still in distress (Follow doctor's orders.)
2. Let victim rest—sit or lie down
3. Apply ice to sting
4. Send for help immediately

Appendix E
Youth Council Standards

As a member of the Youth Council, I realize that my life is to be an "example of the believers," and I pledge to live up to the following requirements, to the glory of God.

1. I will refrain from things that would harm my body and testimony, such as smoking, taking drugs, and drinking liquor in any form.
2. I will refrain from going to questionable places, such as movie theaters, dance halls, and places that promote rock music.
3. I will daily read the Word of God and spend time in prayer for our teen-agers and for others whom I list on a prayer list.
4. I will do my best to come to visitation, unless I am ill, out of town, or have other commitments, such as work. If I cannot come, I will call the youth pastor so that he will know why I am unable to attend.
5. I will participate actively in as many functions of our youth group and church as I am able and will make faithfulness a prime goal for my life. I will also attend the meeting of the Youth Council once a month and do my best to represent the teen-agers.
6. I will listen only to good music and will not tolerate rock music or country music in any form.
7. I will uphold high standards in my dating life and not involve myself in any form of immorality, striving to keep myself pure at any cost.
8. I will be careful of what I watch on television and videos and will refrain from any programs that are geared to sensual desires and vulgarity.
9. I will not be sloppy in my dress but will strive to dress in a way that will glorify God. My attire will be appropriate. *Girls:* I will not wear shorts or slacks in public, knowing that my testimony could be at stake and that I could be a stumbling block to others. I will also refrain from mixed swimming because of the nudity involved and the impure thoughts that it can evoke.

10. I will not criticize the leadership of my church in any way, nor will I tolerate any criticism of them in my presence. I will seek to be at peace with all men and be submissive to those in authority.

Signed _____

Appendix F
Suggestions for Family Unity

A father and mother can improve family unity by working together toward the goals listed below. Each family member who is old enough should determine to list, pray about, and make any changes in lifestyle, habits, or relationships that God directs him to make. The following Scriptures can be a reminder and encouragement to make the right choices: "choose you this day" (Joshua 24:14-15), "according as he purposeth in his heart" (II Corinthians 9:7), "choosing rather to suffer affliction with the people of God" (Hebrews 11:25), "renewed in the spirit of your mind" (Ephesians 4:23; Romans 12:1).

1. Have enjoyable, interesting, and challenging daily devotions with my family.

2. Present a godly, positive, and loving testimony in the home, realizing that my children should see God in me. I will strive to eliminate negative devil-like attitudes.

3. Spend fifteen minutes a day talking individually to each family member.

4. Give one compliment a day to each family member.

5. Have one good family meal together each day where we dine instead of just eat.

6. Maintain a calm, orderly environment with good music, magazines, books, and stimulating conversation to edify my family.

7. Eliminate or drastically curtail and control television viewing in my home.

8. Have a family night at least one night a week when we play games, sing, picnic, hike, or go to special places or events.

9. Start and maintain some good family traditions such as family get-togethers, birthday and holiday celebrations, visiting or vacationing at special places, and traditional foods.

10. Have a yearly project in which the whole family can participate, such as planting a garden; raising animals; starting a small family

business; building a boat, camper, treehouse, deck, utility room, or outdoor fireplace; making an addition to the house; landscaping; or painting the house.

11. Have a special date with each family member at least once a month.

12. Read or tell character-building and pretend stories to my children to develop character and imagination.

13. Have an open-house hospitality attitude and make my home a place where sinners can be evangelized and saints can be comforted and edified.

14. Read one good book each year on some aspect of my marriage or family life and discuss this with my spouse.

15. Turn off the phone or get an answering machine so that I can control the phone instead of the phone controlling me.

16. Get the family involved in some kind of regular soulwinning ministry, such as a child evangelism class, bus ministry, children's home service, rescue mission service, tract distribution, jail service, Sunday school class, or by working with a missionary on my vacation.

17. Try continually to increase love to one hundred per cent in my home, work place, or community by denying self and seeking to be led by the Holy Spirit in giving, sacrificing, and touching other people's lives.

The above are suggestions. It is very hard to keep all these things going consistently; however, it would be good for each parent to check about every six months and to try to keep as many of these things implemented as possible.

Appendix G
Testimony Questionnaire

Age _____

Date of Salvation _____

Date of Dedication _____

Broken Home? Yes No

Mother works full time? Yes No

YES   **NO**

_____   _____   1. Do you have a daily devotional time, reading God's Word, confessing sins, and worshiping the Lord?

_____   _____   2. Do you pray regularly and do you have a prayer list?

_____   _____   3. Do you have a plan for regular Bible study and for memorizing Scripture?

_____   _____   4. Do you praise the Lord at least once a day?

_____   _____   5. Are you known as one who displays a loving attitude by being helpful, unselfish, and giving to others?

_____   _____   6. Do you have good music standards, and have you eliminated rock music from your life?

_____   _____   7. Has God given you victory over sinful habits, such as drinking, smoking, and overeating?

Forming a New Generation

YES	NO	
_____	_____	8. Are you submissive to authority and responsive to correction?
_____	_____	9. Are you contributing to family unity and happiness in your home?
_____	_____	10. Do you possess your vessel (body) in honor and sanctification, e.g., in moral standards and dating? (I Thess. 4:1-7)
_____	_____	11. Are you able to control your anger without manifesting any big emotional outbursts?
_____	_____	12. Have you been baptized?
_____	_____	13. Have you joined and do you take part in a local fundamentalist, Bible-believing church?
_____	_____	14. Do you consistently tithe your income?
_____	_____	15. Do you attend church at least three times a week—Sunday morning, Sunday night, and Wednesday night?
_____	_____	16. Do you invite people to church and other gospel services?
_____	_____	17. Do you carry and pass out tracts?
_____	_____	18. Do you give your testimony at least once a month?
_____	_____	19. Have you chosen a relative, neighbor, or friend that you are trying to lead to the Lord? Are you praying for him, trying to talk to him, writing him letters, and doing whatever is necessary to bring him to the Lord?

YES   **NO**

_____   _____   20. Are you involved in some sort of gospel work, such as a Sunday school class, a Bible club, or a bus ministry?

Most growing Christians are consistent in at least fourteen of these areas and are seeking God's help in the deficient areas. While none of these activities and attitudes makes a person right with God and Spirit-filled, they are aids to Christian growth and a productive Christian testimony. Discipline your life by getting spiritual habits which will help produce Christian character.

Appendix H-1
Religious Survey

1. Name _____

   Address _____

   Telephone number _____

2. Age _____

   Grade _____

   Grade point average _____

3. To what organizations do you belong in high school, and what offices do you hold? _____

   _____

4. What curriculum are you following (college prep, vocational, ROTC)?

   _____

5. What are your hobbies? _____

6. What is your religious background? _____

7. How often do you attend church?

   Rarely _____ Once/week _____ More often _____

8. Who is Jesus Christ? _____

9. Do you believe that the Bible is God's Word and is true? _____

10. How does a person get to heaven? _____

11. If you were to die right now, where would you go?

    Heaven _____ Hell _____ Don't know _____

12. Could I take the Bible and show you from God's Word how to get to heaven? _____

13. Would you like to receive Jesus Christ as your Saviour right now?

    _____

Interviewer's signature _____

Where taken: School _____ Mall _____ Home _____ Other _____

Appendix H-2
Teen Survey

Age (years/months)_____
Sex _____

1. What problem bothers you the most about the future after you graduate from high school or college?

2. What one thing bothers you the most in your relationship with your parents?

3. What do you think you could do to help solve this?

4. What would you like your parents to do to help resolve this matter?

5. Other than your relationship with your parents, what one other thing distresses or upsets you?

Appendix I
Youth Songs

A. Challenge songs—fast, peppy
   1. Assurance March
   2. I Have Christ in My Heart
   3. Dare to Stand
   4. Sound the Battle Cry
   5. He Keeps Me Singing
   6. Heaven Came Down and Glory Filled my Soul

B. Action Songs—rounds, clapping
   1. Jesus Loves Me
   2. I Love the Father
   3. Do All to the Glory of God
   4. Hallelujah!
   5. Happiness Is the Lord
   6. I'm Going to Stand Up, Shout Out

C. Teaching Songs—doctrines, Bible principles
   1. I Believe in Miracles
   2. Maybe Today
   3. What a Beautiful Day
   4. And Can It Be That I Should Gain?
   5. Hallelujah, What a Saviour!
   6. No Other Plea
   7. He Is Able
   8. Lovest Thou Me?
   9. My Hope Is in the Lord
   10. Do You Know That You've Been Born Again?
   11. So Send I You
   12. Nothing Is Impossible
   13. Redeemed
   14. Do You Really Want Revival?
   15. O Rejoice in the Lord
   16. Obedience
   17. Others

18. Christ Has Made Us Free
19. In Times like These
20. Glory to His Name

D. Contemplation songs—on the redemptive work of Christ
1. Alone
2. Ivory Palaces
3. Why Should He Love Me So?
4. Nail Prints
5. Christ Arose

E. Praise songs
1. How Great Thou Art
2. His Name Is Wonderful
3. O for a Thousand Tongues
4. Thank You, Jesus
5. O Happy Day
6. Jesus Is Lord of Everything
7. God Is Holy
8. Praise the Saviour, Ye Who Know Him
9. He Lives
10. All Hail the Power of Jesus Name
11. I've Discovered the Way of Gladness
12. How Majestic Is Thy Name
13. Be Thou Exalted
14. Oh, It Is Wonderful to Be a Christian
15. How Wonderful Art Thou
16. Jesus Is the Sweetest Name I Know
17. Hallelujah, What a Saviour!
18. Great Is Thy Faithfulness
19. Wonderful, Wonderful Jesus

F. Heart songs—wistful, poignant, expressing need or testimony
1. Fill My Cup, Lord
2. Now I Belong to Jesus
3. God Is Good
4. For Me to Live Is Christ
5. Let Me Burn Out for Thee
6. Be This My Joy
7. Do You Know My Jesus?
8. Each Step of the Way
9. His Sheep Am I
10. I'll Live for Jesus
11. Cleanse Me
12. It Took a Miracle
13. No One Ever Cared for Me like Jesus
14. The Mercies of God

G. Invitation songs
1. Room at the Cross
2. Cleanse Me

Forming a New Generation

3. Spirit of the Living God
4. God's Final Call
5. Lord, Send Me Anywhere
6. Softly and Tenderly
7. Have Thine Own Way, Lord
8. I Surrender All
9. Jesus Is Calling
10. Just as I Am

Appendix J
Public School Bible Clubs

- Work in and through a local church youth group.
- Gather together the teens in the youth group that go to a particular public school. Meet all the teens from that public school on a week night (Tuesday or Thursday) in the home of one of the teens. Have them invite their public school friends. The Christian school teens may come to the club if they bring an unsaved public school teen from the high school involved.
- Sing choruses, have one or two fresh testimonies, a short evangelistic message, and then a short Bible study.
- Have food and games after the meeting, but keep the food very simple, such as popcorn and Kool-Aid, or sandwiches, potato chips, and juice.
- Instruct the saved teens to use the survey technique as their contact with sinners and in their evangelistic outreach to the public school and the community.
- Stress the importance of discipleship and following up the new converts. Instruct the soulwinning teens to befriend their new converts and to be responsible for discipling them, encouraging them to be baptized and to join and attend regularly a local fundamentalist church. They should meet with the new converts at least once a week for a simple Bible study and memorization.
- Encourage the saved teens at the club meetings to M&M (mix and mingle) and D&C (divide and conquer).
- Emphasize activism since teen-agers are so idealistic, and God's Word says to "occupy till I come." Initiate projects such as making signs for law-abiding demonstrations against abortion clinics, writing letters to senators or the F.C.C. about cursing, sex, or pornography on TV, or opposing anti-Christian state and national bills. Projects such as these keep teens excited, challenged, and active in doing the work of the Lord and enable them to see His power manifested.
- The teens should be encouraged to contribute to family unity in their homes. (See Appendix F.)

The main thrust in the Bible study should be to teach the public school teen-agers how to win souls to Christ. Bible studies should also be used in a discipling program. Memorization of at least two Bible verses a week ought to be a part of this Bible study. There should be a continual emphasis on these seven decisions, especially on numbers one and four.

1. Salvation (John 1:12; I John 5:11-13)
2. Study the Word (Ps. 119:11; II Peter 1:19-21; II Tim. 2:15)
3. Separation (II Cor. 6:14-18; I John 2:15-16)
4. Surrender (Rom. 12:1-2; Gal. 2:20; Luke 9:23)
5. Soulwinning (Matt. 28:19-20; Ps. 126:5-6; I Cor. 15:34)
6. Sacrifice of praise (Heb. 13:15; Ps. 107:8 and 119:164)
7. Servanthood/Love (John 13:34-35; Matt. 22:36-40; I John 3 and 4)

Because the public school teens are inviting their unsaved friends to the club meetings, there should always be a short evangelistic message. The Christians then hear different ways of presenting the gospel, different verses used in the presentation, and choice illustrations of salvation. These messages will help them in their soulwinning.

About once a month, the various public school Bible clubs can meet together in a big Saturday night rally similar to the old Youth for Christ rallies. At these rallies, the program emphasizes (1) chorus singing with a strong pianist and dynamic music; (2) fresh, exciting testimonies from new converts or Christians who have just won souls to Christ; (3) a good skit (humorous or serious) presented by the teens; (4) good special numbers (duets, quartets, etc.) performed by the teens; (5) a short evangelistic message from a Spirit-filled youth speaker who has an appeal to youth; and (6) an invitation.

These rallies ought to be held in a neutral place (community center, town auditorium) because many different churches will be represented with their public school Bible clubs and their youth groups.

Appendix K
Suggested Reading

Adams, Jay. *Competent to Counsel.* Phillipsburg, N.J.: Presbyterian & Reformed Publishing Co., 1970.

Bloom, Allan. *The Closing of the American Mind.* New York: Simon & Schuster, Inc., 1988.

Bridges, Jerry. *The Pursuit of Holiness.* New York: Walker & Co., 1985.

———. *The Practice of Godliness.* Colorado Springs, Colo.: NavPress, 1983.

Bubar, Paul. *The Jericho Wall.* Schroon Lake, N.Y.: Word of Life Fellowship, 1982.

Campbell, Ross. *How to Really Love Your Teenager.* Wheaton, Ill.: Victor Books, 1982.

Christenson, Larry. *The Christian Family.* Minneapolis, Minn.: Bethany House, 1970.

Dobson, James. *Hide or Seek.* Old Tappan, N.J.: F.H. Revell Co., 1974.

Eims, Leroy. *Be the Leader You Were Meant to Be.* Wheaton, Ill.: Victor Books, 1975.

Fremont, Walter G., and Fremont, Trudy. *Formula for Family Unity.* Greenville, S.C.: Bob Jones University Press, 1980.

Gaebelein, Frank. *The Pattern of God's Truth.* Chicago: Moody Press, 1968.

Garlock, Frank. *The Big Beat: A Rock Blast.* Greenville, S.C.: Bob Jones University Press, 1971.

Gothard, Bill. *Character Sketches. Vols. I, II, III.* Oak Brook, Ill.: Institute in Basic Youth Conflicts, 1976.

Hamrick, Frank. *Ancient Landmarks: A Guide to Personal Standards.* Rocky Mount, N.C.: Positive Action for Christ, Inc., 1980.

Haycock, Ruth. *God's Truth in School Subjects.* Winston-Salem, N.C.: Piedmont Bible College, 1978.

Hefley, James. *God Goes to High School.* Waco, Tex.: Word Books, 1970.

Hendrix, Olan. *Management for the Christian Leader.* Grand Rapids, Mich.: Baker Book House, 1986.

Inrig, Gary. *Quality Friendship.* Chicago: Moody Press, 1981.

Jones, Beneth. *Beauty and the Best.* Greenville, S.C.: Bob Jones University Press, 1980.

Kirby, Scott. *Dating: Guidelines from the Bible.* Grand Rapids, Mich.: Baker Book House, 1979.

Larkin, Clarence. *Dispensational Truth.* Philadelphia: Rev. Clarence Larkin Est., 1920.

McMillen, S.I. *None of These Diseases.* Old Tappan, N.J.: F.H. Revell Co., 1963.

Menninger, Karl. *Whatever Became of Sin?* New York: Hawthorn Books, 1973.

Meredith, Charles. *It's a Sin to Bore a Kid.* Waco, Tex.: Word Books, 1978.

Mowrer, O.H. *The Crisis in Psychiatry and Religion.* New York: Van Nostrand, 1961.

Petersen, J. Alan. *Your Reactions are Showing.* Lincoln, Nebr.: Good News Broadcasting, Inc., 1972.

Sanders, J. Oswald. *Spiritual Leadership.* rev. ed. Chicago: Moody Press, 1974.

Skinner, Betty. *Daws.* Grand Rapids, Mich.: Zondervan Publishing House, 1974.

Solomon, Charles. *Handbook to Happiness.* Wheaton, Ill.: Tyndale House, Inc., 1982.

———. *The Rejection Syndrome.* Wheaton, Ill.: Tyndale House, Inc., 1982.

Stormer, John A. *Growing Up God's Way.* Florissant, Mo.: Liberty Bell Press, 1984.

Taylor, Richard. *The Disciplined Life.* Minneapolis, Minn.: Bethany House, 1974.

Trotman, Dawson. *Born to Reproduce.* Lincoln, Nebr.: Back to the Bible Publishers, 1967.

Wickensimer, Karis, et al. *Family Living for Christian Schools.* Greenville, S.C.: Bob Jones University Press, 1982.

Wilds Staff. *S.O.A.P.* Vols. 1-5. Taylors, S.C.: Hemlock Hills Christian Association, Inc., 1976-1981.

Appendix L
Insights from Humor

Humorous sayings, one-liners, and comparisons can illustrate or simplify principles. Consider using some of these and other original sayings to add insight and humor.

- It was like nailing Jell-O to the wall.
- He drooled a bibful.
- He was as independent as a hog on ice.
- It's hard to soar with eagles when you have to work with turkeys.
- He has the "pooch-mouth" with the grump flag run up.
- He felt like a long-tailed cat in a room full of rocking chairs.
- He acted like a blind dog in a meat house.
- He was as scared as a chicken at a weasel convention.
- That is like having devotions out of a stolen Bible.
- A preacher's belt is a leather fence around a chicken graveyard.
- Chewing gum proves that you can have motion without progress.
- He has a backbone like a wet noodle.
- He came out of college half-baked on his father's dough.
- Running people down is a bad habit whether you are a motorist or a gossip.
- He is like a duck—calm on the surface but paddling like mad underneath.
- That baby's diaper was so wet it had a rainbow hanging over it.
- There are more television sets than bathtubs in America; what a dirty shame.

INDEX